Bookw Dog-Ears & Squashy Big Armchairs

A Book Lover's Alphabet

HEATHER REYES

OXYGEN BOOKS

Published by Oxygen Books Ltd 2014

Copyright © Heather Reyes 2014

A CIP catalogue record for this book is available from the British Library.

ISBN 978-0-992636-46-3

Typeset in Matto and Garamond by Bookcraft Limited, Stroud, Gloucestershire

Printed and bound in Great Britain by Henry Ling Ltd, Dorset Press, Dorchester

A FEW WORDS ...

Read. Book. The most powerful four-letter words in the English language.

The dedicated reader will usually do it anywhere – on top of a bus, under the sheets, on a street corner – though eminent French writer Marguerite Duras confessed to rarely doing it out of doors because '*you can't read by two lights at once, the light of day and the light of the book.*' She advises that '*You should read by electric light, the room in shadow, and only the page lit up.*'

But wherever and whatever we choose to read, it will shape who we are – just as much as *not* reading will. We are what we read in the same way that we are what we eat. Good food nourishes a healthy body and reading is good for the brain – and not just in an intellectual way. When watching television or films, the eyes are mostly stationary: when reading, the physical movements of the eyes (so neurologists have discovered) actually stimulate and condition the brain.

Transforming the brain, both physically and intellectually, transforms the life. Books open windows and doors onto a richer life. But, as a book-lover, you already know that. This little dip-in book is for you: a reminder of the long, wonderful history and the complex life and daily miracle of books.

A

Margaret Atwood – "I read for pleasure and that is the moment I learn the most."

ABERRANT

(Adjective) Differing or departing from what is normal or accepted as standard.

Don't let them get at you – those people who say that, as a book-lover in the twenty-first century, your behaviour is *aberrant*. No. You are a member of a large and very special tribe, a tribe marked by civility, empathy, and intelligence. Its members may not be the noisiest in society, and you may not have another member of the tribe living within a mile's radius of you. But they are out there and, like you, joyfully participating – day in, day out – in one of the most sophisticated functions of the human brain. Reading books.

The motto of the tribe: *Amor librorum nos unit* (The love of books unites us).

ADDICTION

Far safer to be addicted to books than just about anything else.

> **Wise words** 'There's no such thing as too many books.' (And there's no such thing as Bibliophiliacs Anonymous.)

ADVANCE QUOTES

Those words of praise from other writers that appear on the covers of books to try to persuade you to buy them.

If you've ever wondered how the literary movers and shakers get to read the book early enough to comment on it before it's actually been published, the answer's quite simple: the bigger publishers will have 'proof copies' printed and sent out to those they hope might say something nice about the book; smaller publishers, who don't have the luxury of paying for proof copies first, will usually make do with sending the book in electronic form, or 'run off a copy' on the office printer and send it in a Jiffy bag (if they can find one big enough).

Really famous writers differ in their levels of willingness to give advance quotes: some will categorically refuse to do it – ever (or except for friends) – while others are more generous and remember what it was like, perhaps, to be an 'emerging writer' in need of a bit of help and encouragement.

Talking point   Do those quotes really help to sell you the book?

AGA SAGA

A once popular sub-genre of the **family saga**, it takes its name from the old-fashioned AGA cooker, popular in middle-class country houses. The term was first used by Terence Blacker in 1992 to describe certain early novels by Joanna Trollope and has come to stand for tales of 'naughty goings-on' among the middle classes in English village life. The setting is usually a rather cosy one of farmhouses, Wellie boots and dogs. The 'jokey' sound of the term acts as something of a put-down for stories of this type.

AIRPORT FICTION

Not known for its literary merit but judged on its efficacy in taking your mind off the fact that you are about to get into a small metal tube, powered by a great deal of highly inflammable liquid, travelling at several hundred miles per hour, several miles above *terra firma* and that, if something goes wrong, you will most probably die. So it has to be pretty powerful stuff!

ALEXANDRIA, LIBRARY OF

A book-lover's dream … and nightmare. Here's why. It was Ptolemy the First who, in the third century BC, founded the great library of Alexandria. The aim was for the library to contain the whole of human knowledge. The library as total global brain. Dedicated to the Nine Muses and incorporating lecture halls, meetings rooms and gardens – in addition to its vast collection of texts – it can be seen as a fore-runner or model for the modern university campus.

In the mid-third century BCE, the poet Callima-chus was employed there and created the first known alphabetical library catalogue.

The Library came to house nearly half a million scrolls, plus another forty thousand stored in a sepa-rate 'overflow' building. One method of expanding the collection was to demand that any ship stop-ping at Alexandria render up all books on board for copying, after which they – or the copies – would be returned. (Such scrolls were identified by having the words '*from the ships*' stamped on them.) The modern equivalent is the **legal deposit library**.

The main library was for scholars, but Ptolemy II set up an 'offshoot' library – the Serapeum – which was more of a public library.

The library of Alexandria was destroyed by fire around 640 CE: a bibliophile's nightmare. There are various theories about how this happened, but in *The Yellow-Lighted Bookshop*, Lewis Buzbee fleshes out perhaps the most convincing of the stories. When Muslim armies conquered the city, there was a debate about the worth of the library. Caliph Omar's repre-sentative, Ibn Amrou el-Ass, was swayed by the argu-ments of the librarian John Philoponus that, as the library's contents pre-dated the Prophet, they were not 'infidel' texts, and many of the greatest works were of Arabic origin. But Caliph Omar himself was not swayed. Convinced the Koran was the only book anyone needed, he ordered the contents of the library to be distributed around the bath-houses of Alexandria and burnt to heat the water. It took six months for them all to be consumed by flames.

Although there is some ambiguity about the exact circumstances of the library's destruction, destroyed it most certainly was, and its contents 'put to the flames.' Today, however, there is a vast new library in Alexandria (it was begun in 1988) with enough shelf-space for over 8,000,000 books, besides audio-visual and virtual forms of knowledge.

AND ... Alexandria wasn't the only ancient library (though it's the most famous). Other great institutions include the library at Thebes: the inscription over its entrance, 'Medicine for the Soul', suggests that the therapeutic aspects of reading – **bibliotherapy** – have long been officially recognised.

The library of Ashurbanipal, at Nineveh, was founded between 669 and 631 BCE, while in China records show there was an imperial library at the time of the Qin dynasty (around the third century BCE), if not before. And a library curator of the Han dynasty (second to first century BCE) is thought to have set up China's first classification system.

Persia had many libraries, including the royal library of Isfahan and an important public library at Gunishapur dating from 667 CE. Christian and Islamic libraries flourished in the Middle Ages and included the great Sufiya library in Aleppo, attached to the Grand Umayyad Mosque.

Many other mosques also sponsored public libraries which, as 'halls of science', were quite widespread by the ninth century, covering secular as well as religious knowledge. Tenth-century Shiraz had a huge library in an attractive setting of gardens, lakes and waterways – recalling the beauty of the Great Library of Alexandria.

AMAZON

1 The largest river in the world, rising in the Peruvian Andes and running through northern Brazil into the Atlantic.

2 A member of legendary tribes of women warriors, in Greek myth but also in South America. Used metaphorically to refer to a tall, aggressive woman.

3 As a book-lover you cannot fail to be aware of the third meaning. Those who still run small, independent bookshops are only too aware of the appropriateness of the Amazon trading name.

Let's face it, Amazon provides a brilliant service to those who can't get to a good bookshop, those who know exactly what they want and need it fast, and those who have forgotten birthdays till the last minute and know that Amazon can get the book to cousin Jill for you by next day.

True, it doesn't beat browsing in a well-stocked bookshop. But we need both for a vibrant book culture in the modern world. And in one sense, Amazon has done a small favour to 'literary culture': in order to compete with Amazon and stay commercially viable, bookshops have become locations for **author events**, reading groups, and cafés where the local literati can talk about their latest (guilty) Amazon purchases over coffee and cakes whose prices help to subsidise the struggling bookshop.

> **Advice**   Amazon when you have to, bookshops when you can.

ANTHOLOGY

From the Greek *anthos* (flower) and *legein* (to collect). So, basically, the literary equivalent of a bunch of flowers. Rather lovely!

ARMCHAIR – see SQUASHY, BIG

AUDIOBOOKS

Have their uses, but the pleasure one takes in them is likely to depend on –

1   whether you like the voice of the person(s) reading the book

2   how *sensitive* you are to having a voice other than the one imagined in your head reading the book to you

3   how skilful the abridgement is, if it's not the whole text being read

4   how long that car journey is …

Of course, for those with bad sight or simply tired eyes, audiobooks are a godsend. And for those extra long, difficult novels in small print, they can be a real help. I'm thinking particularly of James Joyce's Ulysses. The 22 CD unabridged recording, with Jim Norton reading most of it and Marcella Riordan as Molly Bloom, will, I am sure, make even the most faint-hearted a fan of this Modernist masterpiece.

AUTHOR – see WRITER

AUTHOR EVENTS

Contrary to popular belief, these are nothing new – though it must be admitted that there has been a veritable explosion of them in recent years as bookshops (and libraries) battle to survive the inroads into their trade from the internet, e-books, and the collapse of the **net book agreement** and try to tempt you into their premises with the chance to meet 'big name' authors ... or sometimes more modest, local writing celebrities. It is hoped, of course, that you will buy their books, and any others that happen to take your fancy in the good mood usually raised by such events – often helped along by a glass or two of wine.

For book-lovers – and particularly for lovers of direct contact with authors – these events can fill the gaps between **festivals** with their multiple 'meet the author' opportunities.

But, no, these events are nothing new. Think back to the hugely successful tours of America made by Charles Dickens and Oscar Wilde, playing to much larger audiences than your local bookshop could accommodate. The literary salons of the eighteenth century were opportunities for the cultural and social élite to meet and encourage both emerging and established writers and to keep abreast of literary trends.

And even Ancient Rome had its regular author events. Roman authors began the process of publication with a public reading to introduce a new work. Apparently Virgil and Horace received so much attention at these events that they found it all rather embarrassing. At the time of the Empire the whole thing got quite out of hand and we hear the younger Pliny complaining that there was a 'recitation' nearly every day. As these events were prior to actual publication, authors could benefit from the reactions of the audience – a kind of instant feedback and editorial service. Not a bad idea. Perhaps we still have something to learn from the Romans …

So, when you attend an author event in your local bookshop or library, you can enjoy the feeling of taking part in a long tradition of civilised activity. Do support such events when you can – and be nice to the poor staff who, after being on their feet all day, are still manning the till and pouring wine late into the evening, on very little (or no) overtime, and still have to clear up after everyone has gone. And pity the poor writer, too, who is under increasing pressure from publishers to take on book tours and events as part of their promotional programme: don't keep them talking too long. Just because the person in front of you in the book-signing queue has told the author their own life story doesn't mean you need to. Be kind.

Talking point   What makes for a good 'author event'? Any particularly memorable ones you've been to?

AUTOBIOGRAPHY

A version of someone's life story written by themselves and purporting to be the truth.

The custom of the famous writing about their lives goes back to Classical times but doesn't become an established genre until much later. There are a few famous early examples, such as the Confessions of St Augustine (354–430) and the *Historia Calamitatum* of the twelfth-century French philosopher Peter Abelard (famous for his affair with and marriage to the highly intellectual and passionate Eloise, and his subsequent castration by her uncle). In the mid-sixteenth century, the Renaissance sculptor and goldsmith Benvenuto Cellini wrote his *Vita* ('Life'), suggesting that no-one should attempt to write their life story until they were over forty. With life expectancy much lower at that time, the equivalent today would probably be at least sixty. (Perhaps this advice should be born in mind more frequently by today's 'celebrities'.)

The eighteenth century saw a vogue for the supposed memoirs of libertines – often works of fiction passing themselves off as true and written to satisfy a public taste for scandalous revelations about other people's supposed sexual adventures.

With the rise of Romanticism and the cult of the individual at the end of the eighteenth century and beginning of the nineteenth, and the example set by Jean-Jacques Rousseau in his *Confessions*, the emphasis shifted from the public deeds of the subject to their personal and emotional life, with an increasing emphasis on childhood and early years – possibly a result of the growing awareness of the formative importance of this period.

By the nineteenth century it was expected of the great and the good that they would, at some point, publish a record of their lives, while the late twentieth and early twenty-first centuries have seen an explosion of autobiographical writing to satisfy a growing public taste to learn about the lives of celebrities … even if those lives have not yet been very long. These are often ghost-written. (One celebrity is famously quoted as saying that she hadn't yet read her autobiography …)

The advent of blogging and Facebook does, in many cases, provide the kind of information about a person's life that would, at one time, have been recorded in a private diary to be filtered and refined, much later, into a considered autobiography.

The term **life-writing** is sometimes used interchangeably with 'autobiography' – though, like **memoir,** it may only address a particular period or aspect of a person's life, rather than the whole story so far (which is expected of a full autobiography).

Talking points What makes autobiography such a popular genre? Is there a minimum age for writing a serious autobiography? Are there any autobiographies you have found particularly good or memorable – and why?

B

Jorge Louis Borges – "Paradise is a library"

BACKLIST

An author's 'backlist' refers to all their books apart from the most recently published one. Bookshops are less and less likely to carry a substantial backlist for most authors, apart from the very top-ranking. It's usually a matter of space. But if you want to support your bookshop, rather than buy online, backlist titles can always be ordered …

BAD SEX IN FICTION AWARD

Has been presented annually, since 1993, under the auspices of the *Literary Review*, for the worst description of sex in a work of 'respectable' fiction (in other words, simple pornography isn't included). The trophy depicts a naked woman draped over an open book. The rationale of the award is stated as follows: "to draw attention to the crude, tasteless, often perfunctory use of redundant sexual description in the modern novel and to discourage it."

We won't further embarrass past winners by naming and shaming them: they know who they are … (and some of them are really famous!).

> **TALKING POINTS** Is this just another manifestation of the British 'nudge-nudge, wink-wink, snigger-snigger' attitude to sex? Would the French do it? Why not be more positive and have a 'Good Sex' award? Or a 'Bad Landscape', 'Bad Animals', 'Bad Clothing' or 'Bad Conversation' award?

BAILEY'S WOMEN'S PRIZE FOR FICTION

Formerly the **Orange Prize for Fiction**, this prestigious annual prize is awarded to any female writer, regardless of nationality, for a novel written in English and published in the twelve months before the prize.

Having lost its original 'Orange' funding, the prize was able to continue in 2013 thanks to the generosity of private donors – including Cherie Blair (wife of former Prime Minister Tony Blair) and novelist Joanna Trollope – but the £30,000 prize is now funded by the company producing Bailey's Irish Cream – hence the new name.

While some have questioned the merits of a 'women only' prize, others feel it goes a little way towards redressing the balance for women who can still face a certain level of discrimination in the world of 'serious' literature.

Since its founding in 1996 the winning authors and novels have been:

1996   Helen Dunmore for *A Spell of Winter*
1997   Ann Michaels for *Fugitive Pieces*
1998   Carol Shields for *Larry's Party*
1999   Suzanne Berne for *A Crime in the Neighbourhood*
2000   Linda Grant for *When I Lived in Modern Times*
2001   Kate Grenville for *The Idea of Perfection*
2002   Ann Patchett for *Bel Canto*
2003   Valerie Martin for *Property*
2004   Andrea Levy for *Small Island*
2005   Lionel Shriver for *We Need to Talk About Kevin*
2006   Zadie Smith for *On Beauty*
2007   Chimamanda Ngozi Adichie for *Half of a Yellow Sun*
2008   Rose Tremain for *The Road Home*
2009   Marilyn Robinson for *Home*
2011   Téa Obreht for *The Tiger's Wife*
2012   Madeleine Miller for *The Song of Achilles*
2013   A. M. Holmes for *May We Be Forgiven*
2014   Eimear McBride for *A Girl is a Half-Formed Thing*

TALKING POINT   Do we still need a prize specifically for fiction by women?

BANDE DESINÉE

Literally 'drawn strips'. The term is used in France and Belgium for books in the popular **graphic novel** form, particularly associated, in its early days, with the *Tintin* and *Asterix* series. Many different kinds of texts are now available in the *bande desinée* format – history, biography, current affairs, and simplified versions of great literary works. At their best, they are a genuine art form and, popular among the young in particular, can introduce them to worthwhile areas of knowledge in an enjoyable way.

BAT GIRL

was a **librarian**

BED

Lots of pillows, a good bedside lamp that can be directed onto the page, a non-ticking alarm clock, a mug of hot chocolate, an early night ... Bliss.

BEST-SELLER

Some come and go, some stick around. Some are best-sellers just in their country or culture of origin, others are a world-wide phenomenon. *A Christmas Carol* is an obvious example of a book that was not only a raving success at the time of its first publication, but has continued to be a book that's always 'there'. The same can be said of J. D. Salinger's 1951 novel, *The*

Catcher in the Rye, the initial success being maintained with continuing sales of about a quarter of a million each year and a total so far of over 65 million.

> **TALKING POINT** Which of today's best-sellers might still be widely read in fifty years' time – and why?

BIBLIOBIBULI

A term coined in the 1950s by American writer and critic H. L. Mencken to indicate those who read so much that they appear to be drunk on books. Such people, he claimed, are so absorbed in their reading that they are unaware of the life around them.

We would suggest, however, that being drunk on books is preferable to being drunk on alcohol: better for the liver …

BIBLIOMANIA

From 'biblos' (Gk., 'book') and '-mania' (abnormal, uncontrollable or obsessive desire for a specified thing or of a specified kind).

Some people obsessively collect thimbles … or spoons … or beer-mats … or matchboxes. This is abnormal. The desire to possess books is not abnormal. It is merely civilised.

BIBLIOPHILE

From 'biblos' (Gk., 'book') and '-philos' (Gk., 'loving'). You.

BIBLIOTHERAPY

This isn't therapy to rid you of your love of books: it's the use of books and reading to help in the healing of mind and even body. It's sometimes known as 'the reading cure' (as opposed to the psychoanalytic 'talking cure').

Bibliotherapy has a long history. In Ancient Greece, Plato recognized that the arts were an aid to bringing an out-of-tune soul-circuit back into harmony with itself, while it was a common Renaissance idea that poetry and song could rid one of vexations of both the body and the soul. George Eliot alleviated her great grief at the death of her partner by reading Dante, and John Stuart Mill experienced a comparable 'healing' through reading the right book at a difficult time. D. H. Lawrence said, 'One sheds one sicknesses in books', and in the USA it was used with soldiers recovering after the Second World War.

Something of a 'buzz word' recently in certain medical circles, the actual practice of bibliotherapy varies. At the most basic level there's the doctor's recommendation that a depressed patient go to the library and read up on their own condition, maybe providing an appropriate reading list. The hope is that they will read information and self-help books in order to understand and take control of their condition, with less recourse to medication (mainly for cases of depression or minor ailments resulting from stress).

Then there is the situation of seriously ill people, such as cancer patients, being encouraged – if they are well-enough – to join a 'non-cancer' book discussion group. The rationale for this is that, while it may be of comfort to read of sufferings that relate to our own, a more profound help can come from entering other worlds that help us place our own in relation to them. Better than books that echo our own lives can be those that take us somewhere else.

Some of the deepest uses of bibliotherapy concern patients with severe, long-term mental illness who are being painstakingly coaxed by expert practitioners into language worlds that lay beyond their own closed-in and limiting universe.

And, of course, there's nothing to stop you prescribing bibliotherapy for yourself.

> **TALKING POINT** Can you recall a particular example of when reading has helped in coping with a mental, emotional or physical difficulty?

BILDUNGSROMAN

The German term, in general use, is sometimes translated as 'coming-of-age novel', or 'novel of education' and indicates a story charting the protagonist's development from youth to adulthood. Said to have its roots in the common folk-tale theme of the young man going out into the world to seek his fortune, the term *bildungsroman* dates from the early nineteenth century but was not popularly used until the early twentieth. Goethe's *Wilhelm Meister's Apprenticeship* (1795/6) is usually recognised as the instigating work of the genre, though there are some earlier texts that could be considered forerunners. *Great Expectations* and *Jane Eyre* are two famous nineteenth-century examples, while the greatest twentieth- and twenty-first-century *bildungsromans* include D. H. Lawrence's *Sons and Lovers* (1913), James Joyce's *A Portrait of the Artist as a Young Man* (1916), J. D. Salinger's *The Catcher in the Rye* (1951), Harper Lee's *To Kill a Mockingbird* (1960), Jeanette Winterson's *Oranges Are Not the Only Fruit* (1985), and Khaled Hosseini's *The Kite Runner* (2003).

BIOGRAPHY (see also AUTOBIOGRAPHY and LIFE WRITING)

From Greek *bio* (life) and *graphíā* (a record or account, from *gráphein*, to write). First used in English in 1683 in John Dryden's translation from Latin of **Plutarch's** *Lives* (80 CE) outlining the lives of famous Greeks and Romans which focus on the role played by the subjects' characters in their destiny, rather than giving simple historical facts. The *Lives* are recognised as an important originating text in the history of biographical writing. Shakespeare made extensive use of the translation of Plutarch by Thomas North (1535–1604) when writing *Julius Caesar*, *Antony and Cleopatra*, and *Coriolanus*.

Most surviving biographies from the early Middle Ages are of religious figures, and that's true of both the Christian and Islamic worlds. In the late Middle Ages, the genre was less exclusively religious, and by the time of the Renaissance, the growing move towards Humanism positively encouraged more writing about secular figures. The most famous example of the genre from this period is probably Giorgio Vasari's *Lives of the Artists* (1550).

The first truly great biography of a literary figure, in English, is James Boswell's *Life of Samuel Johnson* (1791), while Lytton Strachey's still famous *Eminent Victorians* (1918) – in which he casts a cold, rational eye over the lives of four much-lauded 'heroes' of the period (including Florence Nightingale) – is possibly the first modern exemplar of the genre.

SUGGESTED READING A list of all the best biographies would need a book to itself, so we're restricting ourselves to a selection of works by acclaimed biographers of literary figures:

Peter Ackroyd has written on T. S. Eliot (1984), Ezra Pound (1989), William Blake (1995), Charles Dickens (2002), Geoffrey Chaucer (2002), William Shakespeare (2006) and Wilkie Collins (2012).

Victoria Glendinning has written on Elizabeth Bowen (1977), Vita Sackville-West (1983), Willa Cather (1989), Anthony Trollope (1992), Jonathan Swift (1998), Leonard Woolf (2006), and Edith Wharton (2007).

Michael Holroyd has written on Lytton Strachey (1994 – though a much earlier version dates from 1967–8), and George Bernard Shaw (he turned the original four volumes of 1988, 1989, 1991, and 1992 into a single volume version in 1997).

Hermione Lee has written on Elizabeth Bowen (1981, but revised in 1999), Willa Cather (1989), Virginia Woolf (1996), Edith Wharton (2007) and Penelope Fitzgerald (2013).

Graham Robb has written on Honoré de Balzac (1994), Victor Hugo (1997), and Arthur Rimbaud (2000).

Claire Tomalin has written on Katherine Mansfield (1987), Jane Austen (1997), Samuel Pepys (2002), Thomas Hardy (2006) and Charles Dickens (2011).

A. N. Wilson has written on Sir Walter Scott (1980), Hilaire Belloc (1985), Tolstoy (1988), C.S. Lewis (1990), John Milton (new edition 2002), Iris Murdoch (2003), John Betjeman (2006), and Dante (2011).

BLOOMSDAY

The annual celebration, held on 16th June, dear to Dubliners and to all of a truly literary inclination.

It marks the day on which James Joyce's Modernist masterpiece, *Ulysses*, is set. The novel takes place within a single day – 16th June, 1904 – which marks the first time Joyce 'walked out' with Nora Barnacle … with whom he subsequently eloped. The main character of the novel is Leopold Bloom – hence 'Bloomsday'.

In Dublin, the day gives rise to great shenanigans – people dressing up as characters from the book (or just in period costume), recreating scenes, giving/attending readings from the novel, and so on.

A true Bloomsday enthusiast will (unless vegetarian) eat pork kidneys for breakfast – just as Bloom himself does in the novel.

BLURB

The term is believed to have been coined in 1907 by the American humourist and illustrator Gelett Burgess (1866–1951) to satirize the excessive praise found on book jackets. The word seems to contain a suggestion of both ' blur' and 'blurt', with a strong hint of 'burble'. The sting has gradually gone out of the term, most people using it in a technical sense to refer to the publisher's description of a book on the cover which, while emphasising the positive and trying to persuade us that the book is worth reading, doesn't go too over-the-top in its praise … though there are exceptions, of course. (See also **shout line**, **advance quotes** and **change your life, this book will**.)

BOOK

Prior to the invention of the Internet, the most effective and powerful means devised by mankind for the spread of knowledge and ideas across the planet.

BOOK BLOGS

One of the advantages – and sometimes curses – of the internet is that everyone is free to broadcast their opinions and experiences to the world. Readers are no exception. Book blogs have added a whole new dimension to book **reviews**. If you're fed up with the sometimes over-critical newspaper reviewers and want a bit more enthusiasm and a personal approach, the best book blogs offer a good alternative. The only problem is there are now so many it's hard to identify which are the best. A few websites claim to identify the best book blogs for you, but there's really no alternative to trying out a few for yourself and seeing which ones appeal. Or, as a book-lover, you could, of course, start your own ...

BOOK BURNING

Unfortunately, book burning has a long history, reputedly going back to at least the seventh century

BCE (when books were in the form of scrolls). In the twentieth century, the most infamous examples were the mass burning of books by the Nazis and the public burning of Salman Rushdie's novel *The Satanic Verses*. Ironically, those who burn books are demonstrating their belief in the power of books to profoundly influence the way we think and their ability to shape the world.

Ray Bradbury's novel *Farenheit 451°* (the temperature at which paper spontaneously combusts) is the most famous novel to feature book burning – though library conflagrations have notably featured in Umberto Eco's *The Name of the Rose* and Elias Canetti's *Auto da Fé*.

German poet Heinrich Heine (1797–1856) famously said that 'Where they have burned books, they will end in burning human beings.'

BOOK CLUBS

Not to be confused with **Book Groups** or **Reader Groups**, Book Clubs are commercial organisations that will regularly send you books through the post – at a reduced rate – in return for a pre-agreed payment. Special introductory offers will often give you several books at a very low price, then a regular mailing of books at a higher – but still reduced – price. General Book Clubs had their heyday in the decades immediately after the Second World War, while 'niche' clubs, catering for special interests, now dominate (e.g. the Railway Book Club, The History Guild, The Fantasy and Sci Fi Book Club and various clubs providing books for children).

BOOK ENDS

A pair of supports used to stop a row of books from falling over. Good gift for booklovers – but do check that the person you are giving them to has no objection to cute owls, kinky dragons, meditating dogs, Superman, and the two parts of a dachshund before inflicting them upon the bibliophile's daily life.

Assume a booklover's taste is simple and tasteful – unless you have incontrovertible evidence to the contrary.

BOOK, ETYMOLOGY OF

The word is said to have derived originally from the word for 'beech' – the assumption being that early forms of written communication in the Indo-European languages (from which the word is derived) may have been upon beech wood.

Happily, things have moved on and we do not need to fell a whole forest for a single copy of *War and Peace*.

BOOKER PRIZE

More correctly, the Man Booker Prize (though many of us still call it just 'The Booker'). So, see the **Man Booker Prize**.

BOOK LAUNCHES/LAUNCH PARTIES

Just as a new ship is traditionally sent into the water with a champagne ceremony, so it is the custom to 'launch' a new book with some kind of celebratory event. Depending on the size of the publisher and the eminence of the author, this can range from a few friends and the local press in a local bookshop (with a free glass of cheap wine if you're lucky – possibly paid for by the author's mother) to a full-scale reception where the great and the good from the publishing and reviewing world mingle and network and drink rather nice champagne. The latter may offer the launched book for free or at a nominal price, while the former will rely on the event for a few modest sales to at least some of those present who will feel too guilty to depart without having bought it and got the author to sign it … just like a *proper* author.

The more modest party – the kind most of us are likely to go to – will be put on pause at some point as the publisher, editor, or just a friend will 'say a few words' in praise of the book and its author ... who may then read an extract. Depending on how well this is done, those present will either be pleasantly surprised or know, with sinking heart, that the book they feel obliged to purchase will loiter, unread, on their bookshelf until such a time as it seems safe to take it to a charity shop or resell it on eBay. But maybe it's a small price to pay to support a friend or a struggling author or your local bookshop, and for a pleasant evening out with nice, booky people to talk to.

BOOKMARKS

Range from the traditional bus ticket to a rasher of bacon (a librarian reported finding such a bookmark in a returned book: I believe it was streaky).

Most book-lovers acquire a sedate collection of 'leathers', imprinted with the names and barely recognisable outlines of stately homes and Oxbridge colleges. These are usually gifts from well-meaning friends and family who know you are likely to use them. (But once you acquire more than twenty, best to cull. Even *you* don't have twenty books on the go at any one time.) The heftier leathers can cause problems with the average modern paperback, straining the spine if inserted on the far left, or just falling out in your bag if not rammed in. The cheaper leathers are sometimes OK, but those with the little fringes at the end tend to go curly and look shabby and unloved.

Easily the most serviceable are the free, disposable little cardboard ones doled out by bookshops and publishers. A happy compromise, or middle way, between the leathers and the bus tickets.

BOOKPLATE

Sometimes called an *ex libris* – Latin for 'from the books of'. They are small prints, drawings or water-colours pasted into the front of books to indicate who owns them. Mass produced bookplates are now available to everyone – there are even bookplates for children – but in their early history, commissioning bookplates from an artist was seen as a status symbol. Some modern bookplates will still use the Latin *ex libris*, but others will use the modern equivalent of 'This book belongs to …'

In Mediaeval times, prayer books would have a portrait of their owner or some other identifying illustration placed at the front of the expensive manuscript (literally copied by hand). With the invention of moveable type and the printing press, and the consequent availability of books to a wider readership, printed bookplates usually featured the owner's coat-of-arms – often in a very elaborate version. Designs became increasingly ornate, but it's only in the eighteenth century that they begin to include images of books or libraries – or, occasionally, landscapes. The latter might feature a memorial stone bearing, for example, the Latin quotation 'Et in Arcadia ego' ('Even in Arcadia, there am I' ['I' referring to Death]) – suggesting mortality as well as earthly pleasures. They portray reading as an activity to be enjoyed (not just a means of instruction or religious observance), as well as suggesting, through the Latin tag, the owner's intellectual status.

Although bookplates bearing family crests continued to be printed, the huge expansion of book-buying among the middle classes during the nineteenth century created a demand for different designs: 'professional' people of all kinds commissioned bookplates that featured their own lives and achievements. By the mid-century, designs punning on the owner's name became quite common, and, from the end of the century onwards, an interesting development was the 'erotic' bookplate.

From the early decades of the twentieth century, mass-produced bookplates became available in shops and the market for specially commissioned, high-quality bookplates shrank to virtually nothing. There was some revival of interest in the 1970s, which led to the founding of the Bookplate Society and two related journals in the following two decades.

Today, packs of bookplates, available in many book and museum shops, make a good gift for a book-lover. In most cases, however, ownership of books – in the age of the mass paperback – tends to be indicated, if at all, by writing one's names on the inside cover or first page of the book (sometimes, not even that …)

RECOMMENDATION For some beautifully produced examples of bookplates through the ages and a much fuller history, see Martin Hopkinson's 2011 book, *EX LIBRIS: The Art of the Bookplate*, published by the British Museum.

BOOKS ABOUT BOOKS

A few suggestions

Breakwell, Ian and Hammond, Paul, *Brought to Book: The Balance of Books and Life*, Penguin, 1995.

Buzbee, Lewis, *The Yellow-Lighted Bookshop*, Graywolf Press, 2006.

Calvino, Italo, *Why Read the Classics?*, Italy, 1991; Jonathan Cape, 1999; Vintage edition, 2000; translated by Martin McLaughlin.

de Botton, Alain, *How Proust Can Change Your Life*, Picador, 1997.

Fadiman, Anne, *Ex Libris: Confessions of a Common Reader*, Farrar, Straus and Giroux, New York, 1998.

Hill, Susan, *Howards End is on the Landing*, Profile Books, 2009.

Jacks, Belinda, *The Woman Reader*, Yale University Press, 2012.

Library Book, The (various authors), The Reading Agency, 2012.

Lyons, Martyn, *Books: A Living History*, Thames and Hudson, 2011.

Manguel, Alberto, *A History of Reading,* HarperCollins, 1996; Flamingo, 1997.

Manguel, Alberto, *A Reading Diary,* Knopf, 2004; Canongate, 2005.

Manguel, Alberto, *Into the Looking-Glass World*, Bloomsbury, 1999.

Manguel, Alberto, *The City of Words* (CBC Massey Lectures), Anansi, 2007.

Manguel, Alberto, *The Library at Night*, Yale University Press, 2006.

Nafisi, Azar, *Reading Lolita in Tehran: A Memoir in Books*, Random House, 2003.

Pennac, Daniel, *The Rights of the Reader*, Walker Books, 2006. Translated by Sarah Adams.

Reyes, Heather, *An Everywhere: a little book about reading*, Oxygen Books, 2014.

Rose, Phyllis, *The Year of Reading Proust*, Vintage, 1998.

Rugg, Julie, *Buried in Books: A Reader's Anthology*, Frances Lincoln, 2010.

Seirerstad, Åsne, *The Bookseller of Kabul*, Virago, 2004; translated by Ingrid Christophersen.

Spufford, Francis, *The Child that Books Built*, Faber and Faber, 2002.

Stop What You're Doing and Read This (various authors), Vintage, 2011.

Suarez, Michael F. (SJ) and Woudhuysen, H.R. (eds), *The Book: A Global History*, Oxford University Press, 2013.

Wolf, Maryanne, *Proust and the Squid: The Story and Science of the Reading Brain*, Icon Books, 2008.

Wood, James, *How Fiction Works*, Jonathan Cape, 2008.

BOOKSHELVES

Never enough. Never quite the right size – especially the 'off the peg' ones. The ubiquitous Ikea 'Billy' bookcases are fine for big books, but they're a bit deep for your average paperbacks and if you're not careful you end up double parking your books simply to make use of the space. Not ideal. Groping for those in the back row can provoke an unliterary – not to say undignified – use of language.

If you can afford it, get a good carpenter to make bespoke shelves to fit the available spaces. There's a lovely volume called *Living With Books* (by Alan Powers, paperback published by Mitchell

Beazley, 2006) full of suggestions for accommodating one's large personal library – though the suggestion of stacking books on the stairs when you run out of shelf space possibly carries health and safety implications ... unless your stairs are exceptionally wide.

BOOKSHOPS/BOOKSELLERS, BRIEF HISTORY OF

Even Ancient Rome had a thriving bookselling trade: the Sosii brothers apparently made quite a name for themselves in the business – which relied mainly on trained slaves copying manuscripts as required (a bit like **Print On Demand** today).

In Mediaeval times, monks spent a good deal of their time – and eyesight – on copying and illuminating religious texts, sometimes to order for an aristocratic customer.

The introduction of printing into Europe halfway through the fifteenth century made book production a lucrative business, and the first great European publishing house was, indeed, run by businessmen rather than scholars: the Dutch Elzevir family ran their company for over two hundred years from the late sixteenth century to the end of the eighteenth century – by which time a good many other publishing houses were thriving across the continent, meeting the ever-growing demand for information, ideas, and entertainment.

In the early days of commercial bookselling, the bookseller had also been the publisher and printer, but this gradually changed and by the nineteenth century the functions had become separate and specialised. In pre-industrial times, printing and publishing skills were often passed down within a family of 'artisans'. But increased specialisation saw the advent of the publishing entrepreneur with a specialist knowledge of markets, capital, and bookselling in general.

Throughout Europe, the nineteenth century saw a huge increase in the number of bookstores – though running one wasn't always easy. In Germany, censorship laws could, at one time, impose fines or imprisonment on a bookseller dealing in unauthorised material. In France, Napoleon instituted a complicated system of licensing which involved the bookseller swearing allegiance to the government so that the bookshop would not become an outlet for subversive literature.

In some European cities, the density of bookshops was such that the modern bibliophile can only dream of: for example, in Berlin, just before the First World War, there was a bookshop for every 3,700 Berliners, and in Leipzig, by 1910, a bookshop for every 1,700 inhabitants.

Just as the first printers/publishers/booksellers tended to be family-run affairs, so bookshops were often family-run businesses in which enthusiasm for the trade was as important as business acumen.

The rise of the railways led to the establishing of the railway book stall – the first (W. H. Smith) set up in 1848 in London's Euston Station, and quickly followed in France (in 1852) by Hachette's 'Bibliothèques de Chemins de Fer'. (The same company still owns the 'Relais' chain familiar to train-travellers in France.) These were among the earliest chain stores which have since come to dominate the bookselling scene. These, along with other changes in the industry, have all but squeezed the small, independent bookstore out of existence. The massive discounting of popular titles in supermarkets has added to the woes of the traditional bookseller.

Bookselling has, of course, changed rapidly with the advent of the internet and the availability of e-books. Online bookshops guarantee rapid delivery, while dealers in second-hand and out-of-print titles can supply a customer's most obscure needs by searching massive databases of available books. Some larger bookshops have Print On Demand machines which can print off single copies of books – especially useful for titles that are not in great demand and saving the bookshop storage space and the complexities of processing individual customer orders.

The rate at which bookshops have been forced out of business in recent years is distressing for those of us who love to browse, to have personal recommendations from our local bookseller, and who don't know which book we want until we hold it in our hands.

However, any living organism changes, and the publishing industry is certainly alive and kicking, though its character has changed in response to changes in technology and consumer demand. But if you are lucky enough to still have a local bookshop, do support it when you can – even if you just buy your birthday cards there …

BOOKSHOPS, NOVELS FEATURING

Not as many as one might expect, given their obvious importance to the lives of writers. But here are a few.

Morely, Christopher, *Parnassus on Wheels* and *The Haunted Bookshop*. First published, 1919. Republished in 2013 by Melville House: two delightful little gems rescued from the past, every word dripping with the author's love of books and bookselling. The first features a mobile book-shop and an unlikely romance. In the sequel, the protagonists have settled down to run a little bookshop in Brooklyn and the plot involves an element of mystery and danger linked with the end of the First World War. Both are lovely, 'period' reads for the book enthusiast, and combine an attractive innocence with thoughtfulness and a good story.

Orwell, George, *Keep the Aspidistra Flying* (1936). Gordon Comstock, having declared war on money, resigns from a well-paid job to seek employment, on a very small wage, in a bookshop … while trying to become a writer. Both ambitions ultimately go pear-shaped, but the story reminds us that bookshop assistants (1) are not well-paid (as true now as in the 'thirties) and may be doing the job because they love books and (2) may be secretly working on 'the novel' or 'the poetry'.

Fitzgerald, Penelope, *The Bookshop* (1978). Short-listed for the **Booker Prize**, this is the story of Florence Green, a kind-hearted widow who, having inherited a little money, decides to purchase an old property and set up a bookshop in an East Anglian coastal town. (The fictional 'Hardborough' might remind some readers of Aldeburgh, whose bookshop – much-loved by holiday-makers – is, happily, thriving.) Set mainly in 1959, it's the story of Florence's struggle with small-town mentality, and the wheelings and dealings of power and politics, as she attempts to broaden the horizons of the local community by giving them ready access to good books.

Calvino, Italo, *If on a Winter's Night a Traveller* (1979). Translated from the Italian, this is a delightfully playful read from one of Italy's greatest authors. It begins by telling us readers that we're about to start reading Italo Calvino's latest novel, so we need to relax, concentrate, get rid of all distractions, and make ourselves comfortable. It then takes us back to the bookshop where – having read the reviews in the newspaper – we went to buy it. There follows a very humorous section about the experience of going to a bookshop. It's great fun and makes you realise you are in the hands of an expert on the whole process of book production and book selling. (Even if you don't read the rest of the novel, read that first chapter and delight in it.)

Nooteboom, Cees, *All Souls Day* (1998). Possibly the greatest contemporary Dutch novelist, Nooteboom has set this novel in Berlin. It's very European in being big on ideas – history, philosophy etc – and, significantly, begins with, 'Arthur Daane was several steps away from Schoeler's Bookstore …'. This is one of the best, and best-known, bookshops in Berlin. Although the novel isn't 'about a bookshop' as such, the opening is significant as the rest of the novel just exudes an intellectual and artistic life that springs from 'book culture'.

Seierstad, Åsne, *The Bookseller of Kabul* (2002), translated from the Norwegian into many languages, this book became a world-wide best-seller. It centres on the experiences of Sultan Khan, a bookseller in Kabul, and his family – and is ultimately a portrait of the Afghan people, too. It depicts the lengths Khan goes to in order to keep literacy and culture alive among the people of his war-ravaged city. His books are burnt by the Communists, looted by the Mujahadeen, then burnt again by the Taliban and Khan himself imprisoned. If you hear your local bookseller complaining about 'trading conditions', maybe mention this book …

BOOKS IN FICTION

Some of the most famous novels in which books – or a book – play a major part include:

Austen, Jane, *Northanger Abbey*
Bradbury, Ray, *Fahrenheit 451*
Canetti, Elias, *Auto da Fé*
Eco, Umberto, *The Name of the Rose*
Fforde, Jasper, *The Eyre Affair*
Pamuk, Orhan, *The New Life*

Schlink, Bernard, *The Reader*
Zafón, Carlos Ruiz, *The Shadow of the Wind*
Zusak, Markus, *The Book Thief*

No doubt you can think of others …

BOOK TOKENS

(Yes, please …)

Back in the 1920s, an English publisher, Harold Raymond, noticed how few books his friends – even the most literary ones – received as Christmas presents. (It was, apparently, a collective total of 3 books out of 119 gifts). Acknowledging that most people felt there was an element of risk (or wasted money) in giving books – did the giftee already have it? … would they like it? etc – he came up with the idea of a coupon to be given instead, allowing the receivers the sublime pleasure of choosing books for themselves. The 'Book Token' was launched in 1932 … and it's gone from strength to strength. The company Book Tokens Ltd is the only UK provider of tokens that can be exchanged in any bookshop, though chain-stores such as Waterstone's and Smith's issue their own vouchers redeemable only at their stores. From 2000, and renamed 'National Book Tokens', they entered the age of plastic and are now issued as 'cards' on which the giver can deposit any amount they wish. The receiver can spend parts of this amount on separate occasions, up to the card's limit. This has obvious advantages over the paper token in specified amounts from which no change could be given if your book was less than the worth of the token.

Today, all chain-stores, regardless of the kind of goods they sell, offer similar gift tokens and it's easy to forget the undoubted origins of the notion – back in the 1920s with Mr Raymond …

BOOKWORM

This common metaphor for a book-lover – one who seems to 'devour' books – comes from the generic name for various small forms of life that do, literally, feed on the binding paste and other parts of books. The larvae of various moths and beetles are among the culprits, gnawing at binding and leaving small holes in the pages. But the best known are 'silverfish' (of the order *Thysanura* – in case you were wondering …) and 'booklice' (of the order *Psocoptera*). One has to admit that being called a 'bookworm' sounds slightly better than being called a 'booklouse'.

BORROWING BOOKS

If you are the kind of reader who will dog-ear pages, drop toast-crumbs into the crevices between the pages (impossible to get out), will happily stand a mug of coffee or tea on the cover of a book, read in the bath (the law of averages dictates that on some occasion you *will* drop the book), leave a book open face down for days so it never quite closes properly again and has a permanent crease in its spine, or handle a book on the beach immediately after having applied sun-oil to yourself or your companion (or children), then PLEASE DO NOT BORROW BOOKS FROM OTHER PEOPLE – NOT EVEN FROM THE LIBRARY. If you want to treat your own books like that, no problem, but do not inflict your habits upon the precious possessions of others ... without their consent. (Murders have been committed for less.) And don't call them hypocrites if you see them mistreating their own books: it's quite different. Think of it this way: we may nag our children about their behaviour, but other people criticising them leads to fierce defence – maybe even blows.

BRITISH LIBRARY, THE

The British Library and the US Library of Congress are the two biggest libraries in the world. The British Library's stock encompasses items from as far back as 2000 BCE and the very latest publications from even the smallest publisher. And now they are also collecting vast amounts of on-line material to put at the disposal of researchers of the future.

The Library's current holdings total well over 150 million items in every conceivable genre from all over the world and in many languages. The figures are staggering: each year a further six miles of shelf-space accommodate something like three million new items. As a result, it's a major centre for research and anyone with a proven need to use its facilities can obtain a reader's pass. Many of its low usage items are stored in large sites in other parts of the country and have to be fetched, when ordered by readers, by a daily shuttle.

The British Library was formerly part of the British Museum and housed, from the mid-nine-teenth century, in the famous circular Reading Room (now an exhibition space) to which access was more severely restricted and for which security was extremely fierce. But once you made it into the great, hallowed chamber, you knew you were sharing the space with the ghosts of the great – including such cultural giants as Oscar Wilde, Marx, Lenin, Gandhi, Kipling, George Orwell, George Bernard Shaw, Mark Twain, Virginia Woolf, Arthur Rimbaud, and H. G. Wells.

By 1997, the British Library had moved into its new, red-brick premises at King's Cross, with open public access to wonderful exhibitions, cafés, a shop, and the large piazza with an outdoor café and plenty of other seating for those who like to sit in the sun to read or eat their lunch. The space is also enhanced by sculptures, including Eduardo Paollozzi's giant bronze of Isaac Newton, based on a famous drawing by William Blake – an imaginative, appropriate bringing together of Science and the Arts. There are also some delightful smaller sculptures by Anthony Gormley.

> **SUGGESTED ACTIVITY**   Go there if you possibly can.

BROWSING (IN BOOKSHOPS)

Surely one of the most delightful and potentially rewarding activities known to humankind. If we always knew in advance which book/s we wanted to purchase, publishers wouldn't spend thousands of pounds having covers designed to lure the browser to pick up the book and many art school graduates would be out of a job.

How many delightful discoveries have you made thanks to those 'idle' hours spent among the shelves and tables loaded with the amazing products of the brains of writers and placed there to tempt you to share, for a few hours, their views of the world, their stories, their knowledge to enrich your own life. Sometimes, you just don't know you want a book until you see it, feel it, smell it, read the first intriguing paragraph the writer has worked so hard to turn into an invitation to join them in their world ...

TALKING POINT   What qualities in a bookshop most encourage you to browse? What are your feelings about bookshops that play continuous background music?

C

Italo Calvino – "I spend twelve hours a day reading on most days of the year."

CANON, THE

Canonical books are those which are recognised as being authoritative within a culture. A work or author becoming 'canonical' means becoming part of human society's collective memory, achieving for the author a kind of immortality – at least for a portion of human history.

The great American literary critic, Harold Bloom, believes that *'When you read a canonical work for the first time, you encounter a stranger, an uncanny startlement rather than a fulfilment of expectations.'*

Each language, each culture has its own canon, but there is also the international canon. We commonly experience works from the literatures of Ancient Greece (such as the *Odyssey*) and Rome (the *Meditations* of Marcus Aurelius, or Julius Caesar's *Gallic Wars*), from France (Voltaire's *Candide*, Diderot's *Jacques the Fatalist*, Victor Hugo's *Notre Dame of Paris*, Flaubert's *Madame Bovary*, the novels of Proust), Spain (*Don Quixote*, of course) as a fundamental part of our cultural heritage – just as much of the educated world beyond our shores regards Shakespeare as equally 'theirs' (to judge by the hordes of foreign visitors who pack into the Globe Theatre …).

By definition, a 'canon' should be unchanging, yet in reality, over time, certain works and authors begin to fall out of the general experience of literature to be replaced by more recent masterpieces. Texts that used to be *de rigueur* for any reasonably educated person (such as Milton's *Paradise Lost*) find themselves largely relegated to university departments of literature – and maybe not even there. Sometimes, though, even if certain texts are rarely read, they have left a residue of themselves in our society: vivid images of the Fall of the Angels – and the Fall of Man – for example, come straight out of Milton rather than the Bible.

There is considerable overlap between books defined as 'canonical' and those regarded as **classics**.

In the last decades of the twentieth century, it was popular to decry the whole idea of the accepted canon of literature – largely because it was considered to consist mainly of works by 'dead white males'. There was some justification for this, but as women were, in many societies, deprived of the kind of education that would enable them to write important works of literature it isn't really surprising. Some believed it was essential to 'dismantle the canon', while others saw that what was needed was an extension or reconstruction of the canon to include voices largely silenced in the past. But to replace Proust, for example, with the stories of Barbara Cartland simply because the latter were read by working-class women seems singularly unhelpful and misguided. Recognising the legitimate pleasure that readers might gain from Cartland is not the same as appreciating the expansion of human sympathies and awareness to be had from reading Proust.

TALKING POINT   Is 'the canon' an outmoded idea? – or is it useful to have a list of works that are recognised as making a valuable contribution to our understanding of ourselves and human experience in general?

CENSORSHIP (see also OBSCENITY TRIALS)

When governments or institutions censor literature – whether on political, religious, or moral grounds – they are, of course, confirming their belief in the power of books to shape the way people think and act. There have been many obvious candidates for censorship, such as the Bible, and works implying criticism of the old Soviet regime (including books by Alexander Solzhenitsyn, along with George Orwell's *Animal Farm* and *Nineteen Eighty-Four*).

Nadine Gordimer's novel *July's People* was banned in apartheid South Africa, but is now on the school curriculum there.

Other famously banned books include Hitler's *Mein Kampf,* Thomas Paine's *The Rights of Man*, the anti-slavery novel *Uncle Tom's Cabin*, James Joyce's *Ulysses* (for obscenity and anti-religious sentiments), *Spycatcher* (for its revelations about the scandalous doings of the British secret service), and, of course, *Lady Chatterley's Lover* and *Lolita* (for 'obscenity').

But, historically, there have also been a few surprises. Boccaccio's *Decameron* and Chaucer's *Canterbury Tales* (both from the fourteenth century) were at one time banned from being sent via US mail in response to the anti-obscenity law of 1873, and even Voltaire's *Candide* (eighteenth century) was seized by US customs in 1930 – also on account of its 'obscenity'. Both *The Diary of Anne Frank* and *The Da Vinci Code* have been banned in Lebanon, the former for its positive representation of Jews and Zionism, the latter for being offensive to Christianity. And in the late 1960s Greece banned one of the most famous plays from its Classical canon, Aristophanes' comedy *The Lysistrata*, on account of its anti-war message.

But perhaps oddest of all was the banning of *Alice's Adventures in Wonderland* in a province of China for fear that its talking animals would teach children to think of humans and animals as being on the same level (presumably because it might put them off their food).

CHANGE YOUR LIFE, THIS BOOK WILL

'This book will change your life' was, famously, the **shout line** on American author Marilyn French's best-selling 1977 novel, *The Women's Room*. But let's face it, any book worth reading should – even if minutely – 'change your life' … or at least modify the way you see and understand the world, even if by a smidgen.

> **TALKING POINT** Which of the books you've read have most 'changed your life' – or enhanced/modified your understanding of the world?

CHARITY SHOPS

One has heard booksellers complain that the widespread sale of books in charity shops is damaging their business. Have they never stopped to think that, by taking books to a charity shop, 'heavy' book buyers are making room on their shelves to purchase more books from their regular bookseller? And, if the less well-off develop a book-buying habit thanks to charity shops, they might just keep it up by patronising their local 'proper bookshop' (an infinitely preferable environment, let's face it) if and when they can afford to do so.

CHICK-LIT

A mainly light, humorous genre dealing with the typical experiences of young women in the modern world. It became popular in the 1990s, particularly towards the end of the decade, with a number of titles in the best-seller lists. The success of Helen Fielding's *Bridget Jones's Diary* (1996) did much to establish the genre – though, in the hands of lesser writers, the genre can become trivial.

Defined by some as 'post-feminist' or 'second-wave feminism', moving beyond the image of woman as victim, the danger is that, in focussing on relationships, romance, and anxiety about one's appearance, chick-lit simply pushes women back into their traditional sphere.

TALKING POINT Is 'chick-lit' good or bad for women?

CHILDREN'S LITERATURE

Before the advent of books aimed at children, they would have shared in the common stories and folktales of their society. There were some publications for children as far back as the eighteenth century, but it wasn't really until the nineteenth century that a substantial literature for children began to emerge. Early in the century, Danish author Hans Christian Andersen collected and published versions of folk tales for children, soon followed by the Brothers Grimm. In 1812, Johann David Wyss published *Swiss Family Robinson* with the specific agenda of encouraging 'family values' and self-reliance. But as the century progressed, didacticism began to give way to more purely enjoyable books for younger readers. Thomas Hughes' *Tom Brown's School Days* (1857) laid the foundations of the 'school story' tradition, taken up later by such writers as Angela Brazil (1868–1947) who published 49 school stories between 1904 and 1946. The sixty books in Elinor Brent-Dyer's *Chalet School* series were published between 1925 and 1970, and Enid Blyton's six *Malory Towers* books were published between 1946 and 1951 (though six more were added in 2009, all written by Pamela Cox). Blyton's *St Clare's* stories have also remained popular. The school story has had new life breathed into it by linking it with fantasy in the *Harry Potter* books.

But the first of the great children's English classics was surely *Alice's Adventures in Wonderland* (1865) by Lewis Carroll, with its fertile imagination and empathy for the child. Like much good children's literature, it's also enjoyed by adults.

Today, huge numbers of books are written specially for children, some simply to encourage reading, some to make money for publishers following a trend, some tackling important issues that affect their readership (such as the books of Jacqueline Wilson). Some are excellent, some can barely count as 'literature'. But if they encourage a love of books and lead children on to a more nourishing diet later, then they will have done some good.

Some of the most famous children's classics include the following. (If you've missed out on any of them, it's never too late …)

The Water Babies by Charles Kingsley (1862)

Alice's Adventures in Wonderland by Lewis Carroll (1865)

Little Women by Louisa May Alcott (two volumes, 1868 and 1869)

Heidi by Johanna Spyri (two parts, 1880 and 1881)

The Adventures of Pinocchio by Carlo Collodi (1883)

Treasure Island and *Kidnapped* by Robert Louis Stevenson (1883 and 1886)

Tom Sawyer by Mark Twain (1876)

The Jungle Books by Rudyard Kipling (1894)

The Wonderful Wizard of Oz by Frank L. Baum (1900)

The Railway Children by E. Nesbit (1906)

Peter and Wendy (Peter Pan) by J. M. Barrie (1911)

The Secret Garden by Frances Hodgson Burnett (1911)

Winnie-the-Pooh by A. A. Milne (1926)

Emil and the Detectives by Erich Kästner (1930)

The Hobbit by J. R. R. Tolkien (1937)

The Chronicles of Narnia by C. S. Lewis (first one published 1950)

Charlotte's Web by E. B. White (1952)

Tom's Midnight Garden by Philippa Pearce (1958)

Charlie and the Chocolate Factory by Roald Dahl (1964)

A Wizard of Earthsea by Ursula le Guin (1968)

The Iron Man by Ted Hughes (1968)

Goodnight Mr Tom by Michelle Magorian (1981)

War Horse by Michael Morpurgo (1982)

CHINA

Some interesting historical facts about book production in China …

The invention of paper is attributed to Cai Lun, a eunuch in the imperial court, in 105 CE. By the end of the second century, the court was making significant use of it. By 610 CE, paper technology had started to spread beyond China, reaching the Arab world by the eighth century, and, via Islamic Spain, reaching Europe by the twelfth century.

The Chinese invented woodblock printing at some point before the middle of the eighth century, and created moveable type in roughly 1100 CE. But requiring thousands of unique characters to cope with the Chinese system of writing, it was less practical than the same invention in the West and therefore had less impact.

However, by the end of the fifteenth century, China had produced more books than the rest of the world.

CIRCULATING LIBRARIES

Before the advent of public libraries, these were the means by which many people found access to books they couldn't afford to buy.

Although there's some evidence of circulating libraries having existed even before 1700, it was only in the eighteenth century that they really 'took off' to become an important cultural phenomenon and a big influence on the publishing industry. By the end of the eighteenth century, there are reported to have been more than a thousand in England alone. They ranged in size from a modest 200 books to over 20,000 available from the Minerva Circulating Library in London.

Subscribers paid a fee to borrow books, enabling the less well off access to wide reading at a time when the cost of buying books was still prohibitive for many people. They were particularly important in expanding women's access to reading and, in turn, women's reading preferences increasingly influenced the books available. A number of those running such libraries expanded into actual publishing and were much more likely than other publishers to produce fiction written by women. Ann Radcliffe and Frances Burney were among the writers to come to prominence in this way, and John Lane's Minerva Press, which operated between 1770 and 1848, played an important role in establishing the gothic novel as a popular genre. The libraries also popularised the three-volume novel – cannily charging for each volume, of course ... with a little extra charge to borrow all three at once, in case the next volume wasn't immediately available (and you just *had* to find out what happened ...)

In the nineteenth century, the two largest circulating libraries were Mudie's (1842–1937), known for providing only books conforming to Victorian morality, and W. H. Smith and Son (1860–1961). Boots BookLovers' Library operated right up to 1966.

But as free public libraries became more widespread in the twentieth century and paperbacks enabled readers to buy books in greater numbers, the circulating library no longer had a part to play in the cultural life of the nation.

CLASSICS, THE

The great Italian writer Italo Calvino (1923–1985) begins his essay 'Why Read the Classics?' with the humorous observation that 'The classics are those books about which you usually hear people saying, "I am re-reading …", never "I'm reading …".' But let's face it, no matter how well read we are, we cannot possibly have read *all* those books that would be included on a list of the recognised 'classics'.

Lots of ink has been spent on trying to define what causes a book to become a classic. Most theorists agree that a classic always offers something new each time we read it: its pleasures and insights are never exhausted.

There are some classics we feel we know by reputation, even if we haven't actually read them. But when – or if – we do get around to reading them, we are usually surprised and delighted to find them to be so very much more than (and sometimes quite different from) the idea we have of them.

But beware: there is a difference between a true classic and the overuse of the term in book promotion. A true classic has stood the test of time.

The literature of each country has its own recognised classics, of course, but some are truly international and we depend upon the marvellous skills of **translators** to give us access to their pleasures.

It's impossible to come up with a definitive list of classics: there are always 'grey areas' of such categorisation. Perhaps the best one can do is picture a number of concentric circles with the 'essential' classics in the middle, surrounded by what we might call 'optional' classics, and, on the outer circle, 'peripheral' classics. Most readers would agree that 'essential' classics would include (to give a few random examples) Homer's *Odyssey*, Milton's *Paradise Lost*, Tolstoy's *War and Peace* and *Anna Karenina*, George Eliot's *Middlemarch*, Jane Austen's *Pride and Prejudice*, Flaubert's *Madame Bovary*, and Dickens' *Bleak House*. But as the world accumulates an ever-growing store of great literature, some 'classics' fall by the wayside and are no longer as widely read as they used to be, so there's no definitive list.

SUGGESTED ACTIVITIES Either alone or with others, construct your own 'concentric circles' of essential, optional, and peripheral classics – or simply make a list of those books you consider to be classics and what makes them so.

Or you could try taking the advice of writer Edward Bulwer-Lytton (1803–73) regarding 'great books': '*It is a great preservative to a high standard in taste and achievement to take every year some one great book as a special study, not only to be read, but to be conned, studied, brooded over, to go into the country with it, travel with it, be devotedly faithful to it, be without any other book for the time, compel yourself thus to read it again and again.'*

COFFEE

Useful for helping to keep you awake to finish that worthy but rather long historical novel your sweet old aunt gave you, as you 'like books', and demands to know what you think of *this* one – especially the ending ... And she's coming to tea tomorrow ...

COFFEE STAINS

A brown circle does not enhance the design of most books-covers and may lead to the end of a beautiful friendship if a borrowed book is returned bearing such stigmata.

(Less serious is that small, brown, tear-drop of a stain on page 22 ... but do be more careful in future.)

COFFEE TABLE BOOKS

The kind of large, sumptuously illustrated books on just about any non-medical subject designed to impress visitors because left 'just lying about' ... traditionally on the coffee table and thus very visible. The irony is that if left on the table during the serving of coffee (a) there's unlikely to be enough room for the tray as such books are, almost by definition, very LARGE (b) any coffee spillage on such books would ruin the look of them and thus necessitate their removal from the coffee table as mucky books rarely impress visitors.

It is possible to be a true book-lover without possessing a single volume that could be categorised as a 'coffee table book' – but don't be ashamed if you have some: just shelve them with all your other over-sized books and keep them away from the coffee. And, actually, some of them are jolly nice, and good for flipping through when you're eyes are tired from proper reading.

COPYRIGHT

Copyright laws ensure writers' ownership of their works and thus an income from the publication of them. Asserting their 'intellectual property rights' is a protection against piracy. Reproduction of even a short extract of their work requires a fee to be paid. Copyright continues for a set period after the author's death – currently seventy years in the UK – so that their heirs or estate continue to benefit from the royalties earned.

The rise of printing and the unregulated copying of books by profit-seeking printers led to the initial legislation in 1662, but the first proper copyright act was the Statute of Ann (1710). In 1886, the Berne convention attempted to establish copyright recognition between nations. Britain signed up to it in 1887 but didn't implement a lot of it until 1988 (the USA was 1989).

Not all countries are successful in fully implementing copyright laws – 'and thereby hangs a tale' … heard at the London Book Fair. A well-known writer was travelling in the East (we won't name the country) when, stuck in a traffic jam, a child approached the car, selling books. The writer was astonished to see that it was one of his own books in a pirated edition. He said to the child, 'But I *wrote* this book!' to which the child replied, 'In that case, I let you have it half price.'

COSTA BOOK AWARDS ('the Costas')

From its launch in 1971 until 2005, known as the Whitbread Book Awards. Costa Coffee (a subsidiary of Whitbread) has now taken over sponsorship of the prize.

With a more populist focus than the **Man Booker Prize**, the Costas are awarded to books that combine considerable literary merit with likely enjoyment by a wide readership.

Winners in each of five categories (best novel, best first novel, children's, biography, and poetry) receive

£5,000, while the overall winner (the 'Costa Book of the Year') is given an extra £25,000. A new short story prize earns the writer £3,500. Twenty-first century winners have been

2000   Matthew Kneale for *English Passengers* (novel)

2001   Philip Pullman for *The Amber Spyglass* (children's)

2002   Claire Tomalin for *Samuel Pepys: The Unequalled Self* (biography)

2003   Mark Haddon for *The Curious Incident of the Dog in the Night-time* (novel)

2004   Andrea Levy for *Small Island* (novel)

2005   Hilary Spurling for *Matisse the Master* (biography)

2006   Stef Penney for *The Tenderness of Wolves* (first novel)

2007   A. L. Kennedy for *Day* (novel)

2008   Sebastian Barry for *The Secret Scripture* (novel)

2009   Christopher Reid for *A Scattering* (poetry)

2010   Jo Shapcott for *Of Mutability* (poetry)

2011   Andrew Miller for *Pure* (novel)

2012   Hilary Mantel for *Bring Up the Bodies* (novel)

2013   Nathan Filer for *The Shock of the Fall* (first novel)

COVERS (See Jackets)

CREATIVE NON-FICTION

A hybrid or 'mixed marriage' genre which has become a recognisable category in recent decades, it applies creative techniques to factual material to bring it more vividly to life. *The Rings of Saturn* (1995) by W. G. Sebald could be considered a distinguished exemplar of the genre. His account of a walking tour of Suffolk includes descriptions of places and people encountered and discusses, *en route*, events of history and literature, combining fiction, travel, biography, memoir and myth is such a way as to make it a very rich and original read.

CRIME FICTION

As far as we know, psychologists have yet to come up with a really convincing theory as to why crime fiction is particularly popular with the most law-abiding and charitable ladies of a certain age who will happily read vivid descriptions of gruesome murders, the murky motives of criminals, and the dangerous worlds of tough-talking detectives.

But it's true that the term 'crime fiction' covers a wide range of stories these days, when even 'literary' writers use the framework of detective fiction as a way of structuring their narratives in order to reach a wider readership (perhaps) – or will actually write 'straight' crime fiction under another name (see **Split Personalities**).

The early works of Edgar Allan Poe are usually cited as the first clear instances of the genre, including *The*

Murders in the Rue Morgue (1841) and *The Purloined Letter* (1844). But it was really Arthur Conan Doyle's Sherlock Holmes stories that made the genre widely popular, and with increased popularity came the development of different kinds of crime fiction to cater for different tastes. Even the basic 'whodunnits' come with a spectrum of nastiness, from the most graphic descriptions of physical violence inflicted upon a human body (or two) to a complete playing down of the violence and a concentration on the psychological elements of the motives and past lives of both perpetrator and victim which have led up to the crime. Some also foreground the personalities and proclivities of the detective involved.

And detectives themselves range from the amateur sleuth – such as 'Queen of Crime' Agatha Christie's popular creation, Miss Marple – to the private investigator – such as Sherlock Holmes, Raymond Chandler's Philip Marlowe, and Christie's Hercule Poirot – and the detective who is an official member of the police force – such as P. D. James' Inspector Dalgleish and Colin Dexter's Inspector Morse.

Many crime novels and series of novels have, of course, been made into films or television series, further promoting the popularity of the genre.

Some theorists have suggested that the popularity of crime fiction springs from our deep wish that dastardly deeds will never go unpunished, that the perpetrator will always be caught, that there are clever, dedicated people working to protect us from harm. But not everyone is 'protected' in time: crime fiction always involves at least one dead body.

The continuing production of the board-game 'Cluedo' is a direct spin-off from the popularity of traditional crime fiction. (See also **Detectives, famous fictional**).

TALKING POINT: What do *you* think are the reasons for the popularity of Crime Fiction?

D

Diogenes – "To own books without reading them is like having just pictures of fruit."

DAVIDSBUND

Or, in English, 'the band of David' ... David as in 'David and Goliath'. Being a book-lover, you are already likely to be an affiliate member of this tribe or 'band' imagined by composer Robert Schumann – a band of like-minded people dedicated to fighting the cultural Philistines. Don't be embarrassed by your membership: wear your badge with pride ... and recruit as many others as you can to the cause (without being a total bore).

DEDICATIONS

1 The author's official dedication of the book, usually to one or more family members, friends, lovers, someone dead, someone famous, or any combination of these. It can leave you wondering about the 'politics' of the particular dedication in the author's life and what goes on in their mind when deciding to whom the book should be dedicated: e.g. 'I suppose it'd better be *For Tom* again – he puts up with so much so I can write'; 'Mum and Dad would be really happy if this one was for them, after all the sacrifices they made for my education'; 'This one really had better be for Daisy, even though she won't understand it'; etc … (has anyone out there ever found a book with the dedication 'This one's just for me' ? – or 'This one's for the dog'?)

2   A dedication written in the front of the book by the giver to the receiver. One of the problems with buying second-hand books – particularly quite old ones – is that these dedications / messages can make you weep: all the love on birthdays and Christmases and exams passed and competitions won and graduations achieved, the once meaningful dates so carefully inscribed – they've all ended up in the recycling facility that is the second-hand book shop. For some moving and sometimes amusing dedications found in books, visit a lovely website dedicated to dedications! **http://bookdedications.wordpress.com/** Here are a couple of tasters:

'*A story about a bag-woman for a bag-woman X*

'*How could I have had such a nice life without you?*'

'*You've helped revive a part of me that was beginning to waste away. I'll miss you, our talks, more than you know …* '

'*May our paths always cross so that on my journeys the shadow of our friendship is a step ahead of me to remind me that it's not a lonely road.*'

'*Happy birthday my darling Paul. May you experience the best life can offer and your heart and mind fly towards adventures of the warm and the red hot. Wish for your peace and your strength. All my love, Mary.*

3   A dedication by the author to the purchaser of the book (or a named friend) available at good literary events and book promotion evenings everywhere.

Pity the poor author. Isn't it enough that they've spent themselves in writing the *book* for you? Can't you just be happy to buy it (at the 'special event price' – meaning the author gets even less, in most cases), go home, and *read* it? But be honest, what you really wanted was the chance to *talk to the author*: you're not really bothered about the dedication at all.

DETECTIVE FICTION See Crime Fiction.

DETECTIVES, FAMOUS FICTIONAL

The most famous AMATEUR DETECTIVES include G. K. Chesterton's Father Brown, Edgar Allan Poe's C. Auguste Dupin, Agatha Christie's Miss Jane Marple, and Dorothy L. Sayers' Lord Peter Whimsey.

The most famous PRIVATE INVESTIGATORS include Agatha Christie's Tommy and Tuppence Beresford, P. D. James' Cordelia Gray, Micky Spillane's Mike Hammer, Conan Doyle's Sherlock Holmes, Raymond Chandler's Philip Marlowe,

Agatha Christie's Hercule Poirot, Dashiell Hammett's Sam Spade, and Sarah Dunant's Hannah Wolfe.

Famous POLICE DETECTIVES include P. D. James' Inspector Dalgleish, R. D. Wingfield's Inspector Frost, Agatha Christie's Inspector Japp, and Colin Dexter's Inspector Morse.

> **TALKING POINT**   Why is the 'detective' scene dominated by male characters?

DEWEY DECIMAL SYSTEM

A widely used method of classifying and organising books in a library, first introduced in the USA in 1876 by Melvil Dewey but now used world-wide. Each main area of knowledge is given a number in hundreds e.g. Philosophy and Psychology have 100, Science 500, Literature, 800. Sub-divisions then break down the subject into ever greater detail, the addition of further numbers after a decimal point allowing an extremely accurate attribution of place. For example, the general category of Literature, 800, is then broken down into different kinds of literature. English and Old English Literature is given 820. The general category of English fiction is 823. English fiction of the twentieth century is 823.91. Collections of fiction in English by Pakistani authors is given 823.008095491. It's a system that ensures you should always be able to find what you're looking for – as long as the books have been put back in the right place. It's all quite logical really! (Fortunately there are detailed guidebooks to help the hapless librarian trying to decide where to put fiction featuring fish by Chinese authors translated into English.)

DICTIONARIES

It's easy to take them for granted. But stop and think about the sheer amount of work and knowledge that goes into the production of one and you will marvel afresh at the capacity of the human mind.

Although Dr Johnson's famous work of 1755 is usually referred to as 'the first dictionary', it is, actually, only the first one *in the form we now recognise* as such. Forerunners – going right back to ancient times – were largely just word lists, often in parallel languages. Some early dictionary-like texts contain definitions or descriptions arranged according to topic, rather than alphabetically.

The earliest dictionary ancestors of which evidence survives include cuneiform tablets of parallel word lists in Akkadian and Sumerian, from the third millennium BCE. The earliest single language dictionary to come to light so far is from third century BCE China. We also have a Sanskrit dictionary from the fourth century CE which includes about ten thousand words and is written in verse!

The mediaeval period produced a wide range of dictionary-like books, across both Europe and the Arab world. But it was an Englishman – John of Garland – who, in 1220, was responsible for coining the actual term 'dictionary'.

The sixteenth and seventeenth centuries saw further publications related to dictionaries (the spread of printing encouraged their dissemination), but it really was with the inimitable Samuel Johnson's massive endeavour of the mid-eighteenth century that we had a 'proper' dictionary of the type we now take for granted.

It wasn't until 1884 that Oxford University Press started publication of the now world-renowned *Oxford English Dictionary*. The twelve volumes of the complete 'OED' didn't come out until 1928. Today, it is still the gold standard for dictionaries and publishes updates every three months. The OED includes examples of earliest known usages of words, as well as examples of different usages of the same word, along with grammatical analysis, pronunciation, and etymology. (A 'national treasure' if ever there was one!)

Another influential dictionary from the early nineteenth century is *Webster's American Dictionary of the English Language.* Noah Webster took twenty-seven years to complete his titanic task, learning over two dozen languages in the process to help him judge the supposed etymology of words. He is also responsible for introducing 'American spelling' into the language, ironing out the historical quirks of many words in the process: for example, English words ending in 're' – such as 'theatre' and 'centre' – retain their French ancestry (though further back they both originated in Latin ... and before that, Greek). Webster wished to get rid of what he saw as 'unnecessary complexities' and make spelling more rational, reflecting pronunciation. (Part of his agenda was possibly a nationalistic one.)

TALKING POINT There are those who think Webster makes sense, and those who prefer words to retain traces of their complex histories. Which camp are you in?

DIRTY REALISM

A sub-category of **realism** referring to a literary movement mainly associated with North America. Its writers depict the under-belly of contemporary life, usually presenting it with detachment and some-times savagely ironic humour ... but nevertheless with a sense of compassion. Economical in expression and avoiding adverbs, elaborate metaphors and

interior monologue, the writer allows the surface of things to speak for themselves. (Authors generally associated with the genre include Raymond Carver, Tobias Wolff, Richard Ford and, in particular, Charles Bukowski.)

DOCTOR/NURSE ROMANCE

Also known as **Medical Romance**. As you might guess, this genre features a doctor and nurse falling in love. They first became popular in the 1950s when it was assumed that the doctor would be male and the nurse female. Even though this is no longer the case, the stories in this genre generally follow the old model. Many were and are published by **Mills and Boon** – nearly 2,000 listed as published between 1981 and 2010.

DOG-EAR

Noun and verb. A 'dog-ear' is what results when someone 'dog-ears' a page in a book – that is, turns over a little triangle at the top of the page, usually to mark the place where reading ceased (in the presumed absence of a bookmark … of any kind).

Readers can be divided into two categories: those who dog-ear and those who don't. (Which are you?) Those who don't will respond to witnessing an act of dog-earing in the same way that a Buddhist might respond to a nasty little boy stamping on a perfectly harmless snail. Even those happy to write all over books will usually find the practice of dog-earing insupportable.

A happier alternative to dog-earing in the presumed absence of even a bus-ticket (or a rasher of bacon [see **Bookmarks**]) would be to note the number of the page and just REMEMBER IT, for goodness' sake!

ADVICE Never ever dog-ear a book borrowed from a friend ... or a library. Please.

DON QUIXOTE SYNDROME, THE

A potentially serious condition in which the sufferer mistakes literature for life. Interestingly, a number of writers have recognised this syndrome and created famous literary characters who have fallen victim to it.

The self-styled 'Don Quixote de la Mancha', the tragi-comic hero created by Spanish author Miguel de Cervantes (1547–1616), spends so much time reading old books about the deeds of 'knights errant' that he goes quite mad. Everything he read in his books, we are told, 'took possession of his imagination: the casting of spells, brawls, battles, challenges, woundings, sweet nothings and affairs of the heart, great storms and all manner of absurd and impossible occurrences.' They all become more real to him than 'reality', and he resolves to become a knight errant himself – both to gain fame and honour for himself and for the more altruistic motive of righting wrongs and making the world a better place. So, giving himself a suitably noble name, adopting old Sancho Panza as his 'squire', turning a local peasant girl (for whom he'd once had an undeclared soft spot) into 'The Lady Dulcinea', and his clapped out old nag into 'Rocinante' (imagining it superior to Alexander the Great's magnificent horse Bucephalus), he sets out on a string of adventures that are as funny as they are pitiful and disastrous.

It's a long way from seventeenth-century Spain to nineteenth-century Bath, but the same impulse – the mistaking of stories for life – re-emerges in Jane Austen's novel *Northanger Abbey*. Spirited seventeen-year-old Catherine Morland is addicted to Gothic novels (perhaps as a welcome relief from the some-what restricted life of a girl of her class). Using their stock personages and situations to interpret the character and owner of the Abbey (which turns out not to be in the least 'Gothic') leads to near disaster – though, being a novel by Jane Austen, the over-imaginative young Catherine learns a valuable lesson, grows up, and gets her man.

A less happy fate awaits Emma Bovary who, quickly disenchanted by her marriage, wondered 'exactly what was meant in life by the words "bliss", "passion", "ecstasy", which had looked so beautiful in books.'

A frequent visitor to the Ursuline convent at which Emma is being educated is an old maid who always carries novels in her pocket which she lends secretly to the older girls. These and other similar experiences of books and pictures shape Emma's dreams and expectations. Her dissatisfaction with a life that does not conform to those expectations leads ultimately to her tragedy.

There are various lessons to be taken from these three protagonists. The first relates to the power of books, of stories, to shape the way we conceive of ourselves and our lives, our expectations and our dreams. Secondly, in each case it is 'second rate' literature that has done the damage – literature that is not grounded in 'real life' and the educative observations and representations of great authors. And thirdly, the Don Quixote Syndrome reminds us that any books worth the time of day should send us back to life in a truly enriched state, enabling us to live in the world more wisely and consciously – and to think for ourselves.

QUOTE 'Reading made Don Quixote a gentleman. believing what he read made him mad.' George Bernard Shaw

DOWNLOADS (see E-BOOKS)

DRAFT

It's very rare for a writer's first attempt at a book to be the version that finally gets published. Most novels go through a number of **drafts**. At one time, preservation of early drafts of novels (or poems) by great writers was much valued by researchers analysing a writer's style and development, and certain universities became depositories for such writers' archives. With the advent of the word processor and the possibilities of instant, on-screen corrections and alterations, this focus of study is less likely to be possible. Researchers may regret this: writers are likely to welcome it. Their art lies in the final decisions they make about exactly which words to use and how to shape their sentences. Would any of us want our first attempt at a broccoli soufflé revealed on 'The Great British Bake-Off'? And it saves a lot of paper and is therefore better for the environment ...

DYSTOPIAN LITERATURE

Utopian literature portrays ideal worlds. Dystopian deals with worlds full of flaws and failures – thrown into relief by the fact that those societies were originally conceived of as 'ideal'. (Think *Nineteen Eighty-Four* and *Brave New World*.) Although superficially criticising imagined societies (usually of some future time), the dystopian novel is used to highlight the wrongs of existing political systems and social conditions. Jonathan Swift's *Gulliver's Travels* (1726) is probably the earliest widely-known dystopian work, while H. G. Wells' *The Time Machine* (1895) is another pre-twentieth-century example. It's in the twentieth century that dystopias really begin to abound – many becoming real classics – with probably the best examples being Jack London's *Iron Heel* (1908), Aldous Huxley's *Brave New World* (1932), George Orwell's *Nineteen Eighty-Four* (1949), Ray Bradbury's *Fahrenheit 451* (1953), William Golding's *Lord of the Flies* (1954), John Wyndham's *The Chrysalids* (1955), William Gibson's *Neuromancer* (1984), Margaret Atwood's *The Handmaid's Tale* (1985), and P. D. James' *The Children of Men* (1992).

By the very nature of their futuristic settings, there is some overlap with **Science Fiction**. Of the many dystopias present in twenty-first century literature so far, it isn't yet possible to identify which will make the kind of lasting impact on the imagination comparable to those mentioned above.

E

Ralph Waldo Emerson – "I find certain books vital and spermatic, not leaving the reader what he was."

E-BOOKS/DOWNLOADS

PROS Holiday clothes don't get horribly creased from all the books they have to share a suitcase with. E-books save paper. They cost less. You can increase the type-size if your eyes are bad, so your reading isn't restricted to what's published in large print.

CONS They're not there, on the shelf, reminding you about themselves and the time you read them when, going about your daily life, you catch a glimpse of the title and author on the spine. They don't have smell or texture. You don't find pressed flowers or metro tickets between the pages years later. Without the physical mnemonic of the actual book on the shelf, it's easy to forget what you've read.

ECLECTIC READER, THE

Definitely easier to buy book presents for than the 'specialist' … whatever you buy for *them*, they probably already have. The truly eclectic reader will be as pleased to receive a biography of Bach as a history of Istanbul or the latest novel from Norway (as long as it's well translated).

The eclectic reader has a wide range of references to call on in conversation and tends to make a good listener as they are interested in *everything*. Their bookshelves are a wonderful testimony to the varied enterprises and cultures of mankind, the glories and horrors of nature, and the revelations of scientific discovery.

The one problem possibly faced by the eclectic reader is the organisation of their personal library. Even if they use a strict **Dewey** method, there are likely to be many categories of a single volume. And any deviation from Dewey (such as most of us have imposed upon us by the available spaces our books have to fit into) will end up looking like a disorganised jumble of books where books on ballet and battleships, telescopes and tennis can find themselves sharing a shelf. That in itself may be no bad thing, however: a glance at such a shelf can be a happy reminder of the sheer, amazing diversity of our human life.

EDITING AGENCIES

A relatively recent phenomenon springing up in response to changes in the publishing industry. New writers (and even some established ones) are finding it harder and harder to be taken on by a publisher, or even by a good literary agent, unless their book is considered good enough to go into print with very little work. Editing Agencies will, for a fee, help the author improve their book so that it is more likely to be acceptable to agents/publishers. This job was originally done by 'proper' editors employed by publishers to work on promising manuscripts. (See also **Literary Agents**.)

ENCYCLOPAEDIAS

… have a fascinating history. Although, in the Western world, there were a number of 'proto' encyclopaedias in earlier times, it's only in the seventeenth century that there emerged what we would recognise as a wide-ranging, organised presentation of secular knowledge – though earlier attempts to categorise and describe the world can provide delightful insights into the world-view of the period.

From the Renaissance to the period of the great encyclopaedists of the eighteenth century, there was a move away from the religious, church-controlled focus seen in earlier attempts to codify and describe what was known about the world. The best known is Robert Burton's *The Anatomy of Melancholy* (1621) which contains one of the earliest uses of the actual word 'encyclopaedia' and, though it set out to analyse and describe the malady known as 'melancholy', it becomes a store-house of miscellaneous learning and wide-ranging quotation.

It's with the great French encyclopaedists of the eighteenth century, Diderot and D'Alembert, that the encyclopaedia as we know it – secular and alphabetical – becomes established. Published between 1751 and 1765, it consisted of 18,000 pages and twenty million words. (Some of the articles were highly opinionated and reflected the anti-church sentiments of many Enlightenment thinkers.)

In response to Diderot and D'Alembert's great project, three Scotsmen from Edinburgh – Andrew Bell, Colin Macfarquhar and William Smellie – set out to top the French undertaking by being more systematic and using longer, more unified articles. Published between 1769 and 1771, its 2,659 pages could be purchased for just £12. This was the birth of what has become the great institution of the *Encyclopaedia Britannica* – which has now entered the digital age and can be accessed online.

The internet has, of course, also spawned a new encyclopaedic phenomenon: Wikipedia.

BOOK RECOMMENDATION   For a fuller – but short and fascinating – account, get hold of Andrew Brown's *A Brief History of Encyclopaedias: from Pliny to Wikipedia* (2011), published by Hesperus Press. Well worth it.

EPISTOLARY NOVEL

A novel written in the form of letters – written either by one person or by two (and sometimes more). With tentative beginnings way back in the fifteenth century, the first famous example is *Letters of a Portuguese Nun* (1669). Aphra Behn's *Love Letters Between a Nobleman and His Sister* (1684–87) is the first noteworthy example in English literature. The genre gained popularity in the following century with Samuel Richardson's *Pamela* (1740) and *Clarissa* (1749), and with Henry Fielding's parody of *Pamela*, *Shamela* (1741). In France, Jean-Jacques Rousseau's *Julie, ou la nouvelle Héloïse* (1761) was immensely popular, as was *Les Liaisons dangereuses* (1782) by Laclos, both still well-known today. The best-selling German epistolary novel of all time is Goethe's *The Sorrows of Young Werther* (1774).

Mary Shelley's *Frankenstein* (1818) is the earliest nineteenth-century example to make a lasting impact – though as we read it and are swept along by the narrative, we sometimes forget it is in the form of correspondence. Some believe that an early version of *Pride and Prejudice* may have been an attempt by Jane Austen to write in epistolary form (the novel does contain quite a few letters, even in its 'known' form). C. S. Lewis uses the form for *The Screwtape Letters* (1942), of course, and Alice Walker's *The*

Colour Purple (1982) is one of the most famous twentieth-century examples of the genre. In the current century, we have Lionel Shriver's best-selling, Orange-Prize-winning *We Need to Talk About Kevin* (2003) and Nicola Barker's *Burley Cross Postbox Theft* (2010), which show the genre being used to tackle both the most serious and the most amusing of situations.

> **TALKING POINT**   What are the likely difficulties for writers when telling a story in the epistolary form?

EROTICA

Or 'Erotic Fiction'. Written with the purpose of arousing sexual feelings in the reader but less crude than pornography. Think *Fifty Shades of Grey* … Not to everyone's taste – but that's one of the great things about books: they provide stories for all kinds of readers.

ESCAPISM

Believe it or not, there are people out there who regard reading novels – even those of the highest quality – as 'mere escapism'. If challenged by such strange specimens of the human race, agree with them. Yes, it is. But point out that it's not an escape *from* life, but an escape *into* life – into a richer and more complex life and range of experiences than most of us encounter in our fairly limited, day-to-day existences. Escape all you can. Enrich your life.

ESSAYS

'The Essay is a literary device for saying almost everything about almost anything.'   Aldous Huxley.

The term 'essay' comes from the French verb *essayer*, meaning to try or attempt. So, an 'attempt' at a subject – exploring it in whatever way the writer thinks fit. Michel de Montaigne (1533–1592) is known as the father of the form and was the first to describe his writings on diverse subjects as 'essays' – though inspired by the work of the Roman author Plutarch.

The rise of the essay form can be linked to the Renaissance with its move away from the primacy of religion, dominating much writing of the Middle Ages, and towards more human centred concerns. Montaigne began writing essays in 1572, and by 1597 the great Renaissance figure, Francis Bacon, had published his first book of essays.

There was a further flourishing of the essay form in the early eighteenth century when famous essayists – widely published in popular periodicals of the time – included Joseph Addison (1672–1719), Richard Steele (1672–1729), and, most famously,

Dr Samuel Johnson (1709–1784). The essay was a form well-suited to the eighteenth-century Enlightenment, with its untrammelled investigation of all subjects relating to human life and knowledge.

Essayists famous in the nineteenth century include Charles Lamb (1775–1834), William Hazlitt (1778–1819) and Thomas de Quincey (1785–1859), while going into the twentieth century we have Hilaire Belloc (1870–1953), G. K. Chesterton (1874–1936), Virginia Woolf (1882–1941), and George Orwell (1903–1950).

Since the mid-twentieth century, much of the impetus that produced essays has been directed into journalism and critical essays on literature and the arts.

> **TALKING POINT** What are the particular pleasures of the essay form for readers? What are the advantages of the form for writers?

EX LIBRIS

1 Latin for 'from the books of' and appearing on **bookplates**, followed by the name of the owner e.g. 'Ex libris Jo Smith'.

2 An Ex Libris is sometimes used as a term for a **bookplate**.

3 A literary bluff game, first produced in 1991

by Oxford Games Ltd, in which players write plausible opening or closing sentences of books whose authors and story outlines are given. A 'reader' reads out what has been written, along with the genuine sentences from the story. Players vote for what they believe to be the genuine version and are awarded points accordingly. Those whose versions are voted for also receive points – as does the 'reader' if no-one identifies the author's actual words.

EXPERIMENTAL FICTION/ LITERATURE

Laurence Stern's 1759 novel *Tristram Shandy* is often cited as a significant forerunner of the 'experimental literature' that only flourished fully in the twentieth century. The early decades of that century saw many innovations in written texts – both prose and poetry – in the period of early Modernism. Among the most important Modernist works breaking new ground in terms of form and expression were the prose works of Gertrude Stein, Virginia Woolf, John Dos Passos, and James Joyce, and poets such as T. S. Eliot and, more extremely, Tristan Tzara, Marinetti and Apollinaire.

With the rise of fascism in Europe and in the period immediately after the Second World War, there was a return to 'realism' in the work of many writers. But the spirit of innovation was kept alive – or brought back to life – by writers such as the French Raymond Queneau and Georges Perec and the Italian Italo Calvino, all members of OULIPO (*Ouvroir de la littérature potentiale* – the Workshop of Potential Literature) who got together to discover new ways of 'making texts'.

Experimentalism was less of a phenomenon in Britain than in continental Europe, but B. S. Johnson and Christine Brooke-Rose are probably the best-known exceptions. (Brooke-Rose objected to the term 'experimental' being applied to her work, however, as she thought it suggested she was just 'trying things out' – as in a scientific experiment – whereas she knew exactly what she was doing and why.)

Even though the most extreme 'experiments' are no longer particularly popular, the so-called experimental writers opened up the possibilities of fiction and breathed new life into the novel, as well as poetry.

F

Anne Frank – "If I read a book that impresses me, I have to take myself firmly in hand, before I mix with other people; otherwise they would think my mind rather queer."

FAMILY SAGA

A novel, or sequence of novels, chronicling the history of a particular family – or a number of connected families – over a period of time, often including major historical events and recording social changes through the lives of the family members. They may sometimes include interaction with actual historical figures.

Some of the best-known 'literary' family sagas include Thomas Mann's *Buddenbrooks* (1901), tracing the decline of a German family over four generations; John Galsworthy's *The Forsyte Saga* (1906–1921), detailing the vicissitudes of an upper class British family; great Columbian writer Gabriel Garcia Marquez's *One Hundred Years of Solitude* (1967), which follows the Buendia family; and Chilean Isabel Allende's *House of Spirits* (1982), giving us four generations of the Trueba family – Marquez and Allende both using elements of **Magic Realism**, which played a significant part in the rise of the South American novel at that period.

Popular writers in the family saga genre include Susan Howatch and Philippa Carr (who also writes as Jean Plaidy and Victoria Holt). Howatch's *Penmarric* (1971) followed the Cornish Penmar family through the nineteenth and twentieth centuries, using their story as a parallel to the Plantagenets. *Cashelmara* (1974), *The Rich Are Different* (1977), *The Sins of the Fathers* (1980) and *The Wheel of Fortune* (1984) likewise use recent family situations to retell stories of the past.

Edward Rutherfurd's sweeping historical sagas also make use of interwoven family histories to document the stories of particular places. His *Sarum* (1987) gives us 10,000 years of history in the Stonehenge area; *Russka* (1991) takes us from the dawn of Russian history to the twentieth century; and he's done the same in *London* (1997), the two *Dublin* books (2004 and 2006), *New York* (2009) and *Paris* (2013). If you like your history well spiced by a good family story and/or want to understand a city's past before visiting it, Rutherfurd is your man …

FAN CLUBS (see LITERARY FAN CLUBS)

FANFIC

Short for 'fan fiction' (or 'fanfiction'), it denotes stories based on existing fictional characters written by fans of the original book, not the creator of the characters. They are not professionally published but are mainly shared online by other fans of the particular characters or genre featured.

Before the internet, stories using existing characters and settings were mainly confined to **science fiction** and published in amateurishly produced 'fanzines' that could be picked up at science fiction conventions. But the internet has revolutionised the fan fiction phenomenon to such an extent that the site FanFiction.net, to which anyone can upload their writing, hosts millions of stories in many different languages.

Needless to say, there have been a number of legal issues associated with fan fiction, though some writers – including J. K. Rowling – are quite happy about it and have even said they are flattered that others want to write stories based on their characters.

FANTASY

A genre that can be said to include many kinds of narrative, from Greek Myths to 'Harry Potter'. Defined by the creation of coherent, imaginary worlds in which magic and the supernatural play a significant role, it allows a free reign to the creator's imagination. Although some would include Science Fiction under the heading of 'Fantasy', most narratives of the Fantasy genre do not use 'science' in the creation of their worlds.

The mythical creatures that plague the homeward journey of Odysseus after the Trojan Wars, the monster fought by Beowulf in the great Anglo-Saxon epic that bears his name, the supernatural elements of *Sir Gawain and the Green Knight*, Dante's creation of Hell, Purgatory and Heaven in *The Divine Comedy*, the 'Never-Never-Land' of Peter Pan, Alice's 'Wonderland', along with the kingdoms of Oz, Narnia, and Earthsea are all well-known examples of fantasy in literature. In terms of modern, popular fantasy, tone and setting is often set by J. R. R. Tolkien's *The Lord of the Rings* ... helped considerably by the success of the films based on the books ... along with *Harry Potter*, of course.

A further development of this ubiquitous genre can be found in the countless video games that use popular elements from fantasy literature.

> **Talking point**   Is 'fantasy literature' merely escapist, or does it have an important contribution to make to our understanding of ourselves and the world around us?

FAVOURITE BOOK(S)/AUTHOR(S)

If someone asks you, 'Which is your favourite book?' or 'Who's your favourite author?', suspect they're not big readers themselves – not in the dedicated way *you* are. Given the vast wealth and variety of the world's literature, how could you seriously pick just one book or one author?

The easy answer to give is, 'I don't have one,' but if you're feeling in an educative mood, you could wax lyrical about how it's impossible to confine yourself to just one when there are so many wonderful books, authors etc etc … Or you could take the middle way and give a few much-loved titles/authors. Often, however, you may find the question is asked because the asker actually wants to tell *you* about *their* favourite book/author (and it probably won't be Virginia Woolf).

FESTIVALS (BOOK/LITERATURE/ LITERARY) – UK

At the last count, there were well over 300 literary/ book festivals held annually in the UK. Small towns and even villages host a wonderful range of events, bearing witness to our thriving literary culture – even in the furthest-flung places. Some are dedicated to specific types of writing, such as poetry, children's literature, or science fiction. But most have a broad reach.

There are a few really big festivals that have made an international name for themselves and one can expect to meet there the brightest stars of the literary world. Below are details of the big ones, but it is many people's experience that the more intimate events of a local festival, organised by enthusiasts, can be more enjoyable than the high profile festivals where tickets might be expensive. In order of dates through the year, the biggest festivals are …

The Oxford Literary Festival – held at the end of March. It has been running for eighteen years so is quite a youngster on the scene. But its location in a great university city has helped to ensure high profile events and good audiences.

The Charleston Festival has been running for twenty-five years and occupies ten days in May. Held at the delightful Charleston House in the Sussex countryside, where members of the Bloomsbury Group used to 'hang out' (the house belonged to artist Vanessa Bell – sister of Virginia Woolf – and her family), it provides an excellent range of events in a modest, attractive setting.

The Hay Festival of Literature and Arts – founded in 1988 and held in Hay-on-Wye (Powys, Wales) in late May. In recent years, the festival has expanded to include music and film. There are also a large number of 'satellite' Hay festivals in other cities around the world.

The Edinburgh International Book Festival – billed as 'The largest festival of its kind in the world', takes place in the last three weeks of August and ties in with the wider Edinburgh Festival. It started life in 1983, in a tent, and was a biannual festival until 1997 when it became yearly. Held in the city's lovely Charlotte Square, it also hosts an excellent children's book festival running in parallel with the adult events.

The Cheltenham Festival of Literature – held in mid October, was founded in 1949 and is the longest-running festival of its kind in the world, as well as one of the most prestigious.

> **TALKING POINT** What, in your experience, are the best – and worst – things about book festivals, large or small?

FILM OF THE BOOK, THE

How often have you watched a film of a much-loved book and wished you hadn't? Film images can be stronger than the pictures in one's head and can usurp our personal vision of the characters and locations. Print and film are different media and the vast amounts of money invested in the making of a film dictate the rules such as that the hero and heroine have to be good-looking and preferably famous. Can you imagine that iconic 'sixties film of *Dr Zhivago* without Omar Sharif and Julie Christie? – even though Pasternak describes the ten-year-old Yuri as 'snub-nosed'. And imagine if they'd included the fact that Yuri settled down with a *third* woman, Marina, rather than staying faithful to the memory of Lara.

BUT it must be said that the huge box office success prompted vast numbers of people to read the book itself when they would not otherwise have done so. The same is true of many great books some people first encounter as films. So let's not be too purist about it.

FIRST EDITIONS

If you are a book *collector* rather than a book *lover* (though the two are not necessarily mutually exclusive), you will probably like to get your hands on 'first editions' of well-known books. These may be regarded as an 'investment'. For the plain book *lover*, however, the value of a book will reside in its contents, and the investment made in terms of time given to reading it. The 'return' on such an investment cannot be measured, and in many instances cannot even be described. Who can give a monetary value to the beauties of *The Odyssey*, the wit of Jane Austen or Laurence Sterne, the wisdom of George Eliot, the indignation of Dickens, the exquisite prose of Virginia Woolf, the delights of Winnie-the-Pooh. Beauty, wit, wisdom, inspiration, charm and delight do not depend upon the date the book was printed, nor upon the condition of the cover or endpapers – though a *beautiful* version (first edition or not) of a great or favourite book is always a source of added pleasure, of course.

FIRST PERSON NARRATIVE

The technical name for a story written as from the protagonist's direct experience, using the pronoun 'I'. It's a device that can make it easier for the reader to identify with the protagonist and has become particularly prevalent in recent decades – though it has a long history: think of *Robinson Crusoe* (1719), *Tristram Shandy* (1759–1767), *David Copperfield* (1850), *Great Expectations* (1861), *Catcher in the Rye* (1951), *To Kill a Mockingbird* (1960). One of the possible drawbacks of first person narrative is that the author can only include what the narrator would know, therefore the reader only gets one side of the story and thus limited information. But this is usually a small price to pay for the immediacy of experiencing the story in a very direct way and feeling a sense of deep identification with the narrating character.

> **TALKING POINT** Referring to examples of novels written as first person narrative that you know well, consider how different they would be if written as **third person narrative**.

FOXED/FOXING/SLIGHTLY FOXED

'Foxing' is the term used for the age-related spots and patches of a reddish-brown colour (yes, fox-coloured) that affects old paper. It is thought to be caused either by a fungus or, more probably, the oxidisation over time of iron or some other substance in the materials from which the paper was made. In the world of antiquarian book collecting, 'foxing' can reduce a book's value, even though it doesn't actually destroy the paper: it just looks a bit 'orrible. Books affected are said to be 'slightly foxed' or 'heavily foxed'.

The term 'Slightly Foxed' has been adopted by an independent literary journal and their related book imprint – which also has a delicious little bookshop on London's Gloucester Road (number 123), selling a mixture of new and old books. Definitely worth checking out if you're in the area. (Still there at the time of writing.)

FUN AND GAMES

…or literature playing with itself.

Any writer worth their salt is well read, and some so enjoy living with other writers' creations that they can't resist writing about them. This is beyond the subtle, inter-textual referencing that happens in many a sophisticated novel: take, for example, Jasper Fforde's 2001 novel *The Eyre Affair* (that's Eyre as in Jane Eyre) – a fantasy science-fiction mystery, set in an 'alternative' 1985, in which the literary detective Thursday Next is able to enter fictional worlds. (A lovely, rumbustious romp of a book.) Matthew Pearl's *The Dante Club* (2004) is set at the time of the American Civil War. Some well-known poets, engaged in translating Dante's *Inferno*, notice that the circumstances of a series of murders correspond chillingly to punishments imposed on the damned in that book. In Christine Brooke-Rose's wonderfully witty carnival of a novel, *Textermination* (1991), a vast array of literary characters from many periods and places travel to a 'Literary Convention' in San Francisco to try to prevent the gradual 'extermination' of the texts they appear in. Though freed from their original stories, they continue to be true to their characters: Humbert Humbert (from Nabokov's *Lolita*) has designs on Henry James' Maisie (from *What Maisie Knew*); Sir Lancelot and Emma Bovary manage some heavy petting during a sightseeing trip to Death Valley; and *Moby Dick*'s Captain Ahab is helped onto the tour bus by Odysseus and Leopold Bloom.

Then there are the games writers play with the language itself, undoubtedly the most remarkable being French writer Georges Perec's *La Disparition* (1969) – a **lipogram** in the form of a whole novel written entirely without the letter 'e'. Perec, along with the famous French novelist Raymond Queneau, was a member of OULIPO, a group dedicated to finding new ways of making fiction. (See under **Experimental fiction**.)

G

William Gladstone – "Without the blessing of reading, the burden of life would ... almost be intolerable, and the riches of life would be reduced to the merest penury."

GAMES TO PLAY WITH BOOKS

Reading doesn't *have* to be a solitary, anti-social activity – as members of reader groups will tell you. Yes, there's a time for curling up, in silence, with an all-involving tome. But you can also find new books and new pleasures with the help of games such as those suggested below.

Book tasting Invite some booky friends round – between three and seven is ideal – and ask them each to bring two or three books they think others might not have read. They don't have to be 'favourite' books: they could be 'loathed' books, or books never finished. Over tea and cakes – or wine and 'nibbles' – taste each other's literary offerings. A good way to try something new and maybe discover pleasures you might otherwise have missed.

Musical books (c.f. Musical chairs) Another small-group activity. The number of books match the number of participants, and, ideally, the books should be unknown to the participants. (Good to have some 'spares' for those who have read just about everything!) The books are distributed at random. Decide a time limit for each reading – ten minutes is about right. Everyone reads in silence and without comment. At the end of the agreed time, each person notes down the title, author, and their response to the opening before passing the book to the person on their left (or right). Repeat for as many books/ people in the group … or until you are running out of time. At the end, spend some time comparing reactions to what you've read and say whether the openings have persuaded you to try the whole book.

The Grand Tour Gentlemen of the eighteenth century would complete their education by going on a 'Grand Tour' of certain European countries – mainly Italy, France, Germany, and sometimes Greece. As well as cultural knowledge, they would bring back art and other treasures. It's easy to do a literary version of the 'Grand Tour', but unless you have a large collection of unread books translated from European languages, this game is best played in a library – either alone or with a discreet companion. Find the section of the library that houses European fiction: Dewey Decimal numbers for Germanic literature are the 830 section; for French, 840; for Italian, 850; for Spanish, Portuguese and South American literature, 860. Choose one or more books from each country. Read the openings of a few books, along with the blurbs and biographies of the writers (if included) and see if any cultural riches take your fancy. Take them home with you! You could, of course, extend this to a **World Tour** and try books translated from Chinese or Japanese, for example. It's a cheap way of seeing the world – and no airport security personnel making you take your shoes off.

Starlight Express   Before you get into bed, grab a book that's been lurking, unread, on your shelves – or a book you haven't read for a long time – and simply open it and read for however long you can stay awake. Next morning, put it back on the shelf – unless so inspired that you just *have* to read the rest. That night, take down a different book … Simply getting a quick taste of a writer or book in this way can be fun and rewarding, especially if your time for reading is limited.

Blurb It   The descriptive 'blurbs' on the backs of books don't always correspond with our own views of the book or the particular pleasures it affords. Try summing up your reactions to books by rewriting the blurbs. In a reader group situation where everyone has read the same book, comparing those rewritten blurbs can be a way in to discussing the book itself.

Ballooning Using the principle of the 'balloon debate' (a hot-air balloon will crash unless one passenger is thrown over the side, so each has to argue the case for their own survival), choose four or five well-known books and, comparing their merits, decide which one could be most easily lost to posterity …

GENRE FICTION

Sometimes called 'category fiction', is written to conform to certain expectations familiar to regular readers of a particular genre – such as **Science Fiction**, **Crime Fiction**, **Fantasy** etc. It is usually differentiated from 'literary fiction', although there can be no hard and fast boundaries between the two. Margaret Atwood's *The Handmaid's Tale* (1985), for example, is both 'literary' and Science Fiction.

The evolution of some genres seem to have sprung from particular works. The stories of Edgar Alan Poe are often cited as giving birth to the 'mystery' and 'horror' genres; Mary Shelley's *Frankenstein* (1818) is sometimes considered the first work of science fiction – though Jules Verne and H. G. Wells are the more considerable establishers of the genre.

As each genre has evolved over time, most have divided into a number of recognisable sub-genres e.g. Fantasy may be 'low fantasy', in which realistic elements are a significant feature, or 'high fantasy', set in a totally fictitious, constructed world.

Larger bookshops will have shelf-space dedicated to specific genres so that fans of a particular genre can locate books easily. At its worst, genre fiction is formulaic and imitative, but in the hands of a good writer, any genre can become a vehicle for an interesting, imaginative, and mind-expanding reading experience.

GENTLEMAN PUBLISHER

Some would call this a 'dying breed' – others would say the funeral was already some time ago. The term reminds us of another age, when books were considered the very stuff of civilised life, rather than a mega industry run primarily for profit. The term 'gentleman publisher' conjures the image of a person whose independent means and faith in the importance of good books enabled him (and it usually was a 'him') to indulge his passion for publishing. He may not have made a fortune out of the enterprise and may, indeed, have become a little shabby and unworldly as a result of his dedication.

He is not just a British phenomenon: for example, Roger W. Straus Jnr (1917–2004) – of the famous

US publisher Farrar, Straus and Giroux – has been called 'the last of the gentleman publishers' ... though, according to those who knew him, he was a more brash and opinionated version of the typical British example of the phenomenon. But he perhaps spoke for all of his kind in his criticism of the giant publishing houses as being run by accountants, business-men and lawyers who have very little concern for 'the book' and that they "could just as easily be selling string, spaghetti or rugs." The over-hyping of books was another of his *bêtes noires*.

The best British example I can think of is the wonderful Victor Gollanz.

Happily, one of the inadvertent results of publishing becoming largely the realm of big business (it's said that marketing departments, rather than editors, now decide which books the big companies will take on) is the emergence of a modern form of the 'gentleman publisher' – though it is just as likely to be a 'lady' publisher. The wealth of small presses springing up, like tiny green plants between the hefty paving slabs of the publishing conglomerates, are dedicated to making available the many excellent books that the profit-driven giants of the book world will not take on. These new versions of the gentleman publisher may not be persons of large, independent means, but will be good at securing grants or devising a regular income from subscribers, or other means, and, full of passion, commitment, and energy – and a good knowledge of how to use the Web for promotion – are enriching our book culture in the face of those piles of celebrity biographies you have to squeeze past in the usual chain-store.

So, phoenix-like, the 'gentleman publisher' has risen again – though less likely to smell of port and good pipe tobacco.

GHOST WRITERS/GHOSTING

Are you a busy celebrity? … or a celebrity who finds it … er …a bit difficult to … er … put things into … er … words? Then you need a ghost-writer to write your autobiography for you. Some ghost-writers work closely with their subject so that the process is a truly collaborative one. Others just get on with the job (which can pay quite well …). But – as mentioned under **Autobiography** – do not be caught out as one celebrity was, inadvertently letting slip that she hadn't yet read her autobiography …

GIFT BOOKS

A possible alternative to a decent box of chocolates. A light-hearted, smallish, ideally attractive-looking stocking-filler (a bit like this book, really) that makes the ideal birthday present for a bibliophile friend who already has everything in the way of 'proper' literature from the *Gilgamesh* to all the works of the latest Nobel Prize winner. You want to acknowledge their love of books by giving them one but know that a happy little dip-in volume will be welcomed as a bit of light relief because they're currently trying to keep ahead of the judges by reading their way through the entire Man Booker long-list.

GIFTS, BOOKS AS

Giving books as gifts is a wonderful thing – but also a minefield. If the recipient is a dedicated book-lover already, the chances are they will already have the book you have so thoughtfully chosen as 'just right' for them. If not already a book-lover, choosing to give a book can appear as flaunting your superior cultural status. Somewhere between the two lies the usual dilemma of trying to pitch your choice at just the right level so the recipient feels neither insulted nor under pressure. You could always solve the problem by asking if there is a particular book they would like ... or just play it safe and give a **book token ...** or a really nice box of chocolates.

GOTHIC FICTION/GOTHIC HORROR

Bear in mind that the German term for it is *Schauerroman* – 'shudder novel' – and you'll get the picture.

The genre emerged during the second half of the eighteenth century – some say as a reaction against the Enlightenment's 'good sense and clarity' – but became particularly strong during the nineteenth century.

Taking its name from the 'Gothic' crumbling castles, abbeys and creepy old houses in which the stories were set, the genre's invention is usually attributed to Horace Walpole, the second edition of whose 1764 novel *The Castle of Otranto*, bore the sub-title 'A Gothic story'. Walpole's stated aim was to combine the Mediaeval romance with the modern novel which he felt was being overly limited by its preoccupation with everyday life and manners and didn't acknowledge or give scope for the often violent feelings and ideas of the imagination. *The Castle of Otranto* was full of ghosts, statues dripping blood, trapdoors leading to a terrifying maze of underground passages and mysterious giants in armour.

Characterised by melodrama, by virtuous maidens confronted by tyrannous villains and the inevitable courageous hero, and by a standard cast of support 'types' (often including a silly old woman, a stupid servant, and maybe a rather weak or suspect member of the clergy, and sometimes a bandit or two), the source of the genre's popularity among certain sorts of readers seems to have been the *frisson* of terror it could provide.

The influence of Gothic novels on the imagination of Catherine Morland in Jane Austen's posthumously published *Northanger Abbey* (1818) leads to an amusing confrontation between the features of the literary genre and real life – the result of muddling the two almost leading to disaster.

As well as *The Castle of Otranto*, Catherine was familiar with Ann Radcliffe's *The Mysteries of Udolpho* (1794) – the most famous of her best-selling titles in the genre and which spawned many imitators.

The stories of Edgar Alan Poe, along with Mary Shelley's *Frankenstein* (1818) and Bram Stoker's *Dracula* (1897) are scarcely imaginable without the earlier Gothic novels, while Robert Louis Stevenson's *Strange Case of Dr Jekyll and Mr Hyde* (1886), Oscar Wilde's *Picture of Dorian Gray* (1891) and Henry James's *Turn of the Screw* (1898) also owe a great deal to the genre – as does Gaston Leroux's *Phantom of the Opera* (serialised 1909–1910). Charlotte Brontë's *Jane Eyre* and the works of Daphne du Maurier also reflect Gothic tendencies, and the genre can be seen as the forerunner of modern **Horror** fiction and of **Southern Gothic**.

GRAPHIC NOVEL

Has only become a recognised bookshop category since the start of this century, although the term goes back to the 1960s. But publications linking narrative text with illustrations have a much longer history and are familiar through comic books and magazines. It has even been suggested that some of the narratives of William Blake (1757–1826), in which words and pictures are linked, are early precursors of the genre – and maybe the Bayeux Tapestry, sewn shortly after 1066, and telling the story of William the Conqueror's invasion of Britain, would qualify as an even earlier example.

The graphic novel has long been popular in France and Belgium with series such as *The Adventures of Tintin* and the many books in the *Asterix* series. In Britain, Raymond Briggs' best-selling books in graphic form, *Father Christmas* (1972), *The Snowman* (1978), and the much darker *When the Wind Blows* (1982) did much to popularise the form. Though intended for children, they were much enjoyed by adults and *When the Wind Blows*, dealing with the effects of nuclear war, clearly demonstrated that it could be used effectively for more adult material. And in 1986, the publication of *Maus*, by American Art Spiegelman, was further evidence that this could be a sophisticated adult genre. (It even won a Pulitzer Prize.)

The growing popularity of the graphic novel may be linked to the fact that we are (so we're told) becoming an increasingly 'visual' culture.

Not all the books found on bookshop shelves under the category of 'Graphic Novels' are actually 'novels' in the usual sense. Biographies and books on all sorts of topics appear under the label, and the artwork is becoming increasingly sophisticated. The genre is particularly popular with the young. (See also **Manga**.)

H

Mark Haddon – "Books are like people. Some look deceptively attractive from a distance, some deceptively unappealing; some are easy company, some demand hard work that isn't guaranteed to pay off. Some become friends and stay friends for life."

HADRIAN, LIBRARY OF

Built by the Roman emperor Hadrian in Athens in 131/132 C.E, it lies just north of the Roman Agora, which is itself on the north side of the Acropolis. Although known as the Library, it was really a multi-purpose cultural centre enhanced by a pleasant garden with a pool. As well as a public space in which to relax, the citizens of Athens could enjoy works of art, listen to lectures in the lecture halls and, of course, make use of the library and reading rooms. The remains of the complex can still be seen in Athens and, with a little imagination, one can conjure a picture of what it used to be: white marble columns sparkling in the Mediterranean sunlight, the blue sky, the plash of water and the scent of flowers … (Your local library?? …)

HAIRDRESSERS

For female book-lovers, the hairdressing salon provides an opportunity for a little low-grade missionary work on behalf of 'the book'. When the girl who sweeps the hair and makes the tea asks, 'Can I get you a magazine?', say, sweetly, 'No, I don't need one, thank you: I have a book with me.'

HAPPY HOUR

Come on, bookaholics, let's wrest the term away from the alcoholics. Rose Macaulay – author of *The Towers of Trebizond* (1956) – said that there was only one hour better than the one spent reading in bed before sleeping: the hour spent in bed, with a book, before getting up.

HARDBACKS

Until relatively recently, most books were published in hardback before 'going into' paperback, usually a year after original publication. This is still sometimes the case, but increasingly books are skipping the more expensive hardback stage and appearing in the cheaper paperback format straight away.

Libraries were previously the big customers for the hardback edition, but that is no longer the case. Paperbacks are now more hard-wearing than they used to be and are often preferred by library users as they are less heavy and less bulky.

An advantage of most hardback editions is that the typeface and spacing tends to be more generous and thus easier on the eyes. For those who employ e-readers, this is no longer an issue as type size can be controlled to suit one's eyesight.

But it's still nice to give – and receive – the occasional hardback. It can lend a book a measure of 'gravitas', perhaps?

HARDBOILED

A sub-genre of **crime fiction**, characterised by the unsentimental, tough (like a hardboiled egg, presumably …), cynical attitude of the detective. Two famous examples are Dashiel Hammett's *The Maltese Falcon* (1929), featuring private eye Sam Spade, and Raymond Chandler's *The Big Sleep* (1939), featuring the detective Philip Marlowe. (Chandler admitted the influence of Hammett.) Hardboiled crime fiction particularly flourished in the USA between the 1930s and 1950s.

HAY

Common abbreviation of **Hay-on-Wye**.

HAY-ON-WYE

Twinned with Timbuktu.

… Oh, yes, and also home of the wonderful **Hay Festival** of Literature and Arts which Bill Clinton, no doubt recalling his happy hippy youth, described as 'the Woodstock of the mind'. (Get there if you can: it's in Wales.) Founded in 1988, it has been variously sponsored by the *Guardian*, the *Sunday Times* and the *Telegraph*. Originally focussing just on literature, it now includes other art forms such as music and film, as well as a children's festival ('Hay Fever'), and has spawned sister festivals in locations across the world – including Beirut, Belfast, Bogota, Dhaka, the Maldives, Nairobi, Segovia and Xalapa.

HEAVY

With regard to books, this adjective is applied to (a) the actual weight of a book – such as the large print version of *War and Peace* (b) the more than usually demanding nature of a book's content, which will differ from reader to reader but is likely to include a number of German classics of the early twentieth century.

HISTORICAL FICTION

Even before Hilary Mantel came along with *Wolf Hall* and *Bring up the Bodies*, historical fiction was one of the most popular genres. Attempting to recreate events, societies and individuals from the past, it is usually reckoned that the author needs to be writing about a period at the very least twenty-five years before the time of composition, and much of the most popular historical fiction goes back much further. Such novels are often admired for the extent and accuracy of the research necessary, as well as the writer's ability to tell an involving story and to give a convincing flavour and texture of what life was like at the time.

Good historical novels can be the most palatable way of learning about the past, and many writers specialise in particular periods and/or locations. Georgette Heyer helped establish the 'historical romance' genre, and its subgenre the 'Regency romance', for example. Jean Plaidy (who also wrote as Victoria Holt and under other names, too) specialised in the fictionalised history of European royalty, Philippa Gregory has written a lot about the Tudor court, and Mary Renault is well-known for her books set in Ancient Greece.

Some writers not specialising in the genre have written outstanding historical novels, such as poet Robert Graves – whose *I, Claudius* and *Claudius the God* are famous portrayals of life in Ancient Rome – and Charles Dickens. His *A Tale of Two Cities* is possibly the most famous fictional portrayal of the Terror after the French Revolution of 1789.

HORROR

1 Prospect of a long journey without a book.

2 Permanent closure of your local library/favourite bookshop (or threat thereof).

3 A genre of fiction designed to frighten or so appal the reader that nightmares are the likely outcome for the more sensitive reader.

4 Stories that make you prefer your own life and situation, even if it is a bit boring ...

TALKING POINT Do horror stories damage or enhance our imagination in a valuable way?

I

Italian Proverb – "There is no worse robber than a bad book."

IDENTIFYING WITH CHARACTERS

Many people can't read a book unless it contains a character they can 'identify with'. This starts in childhood, of course – probably with Alice in *Alice in Wonderland*, Mole in *The Wind in the Willows*, probably George in *The Famous Five* stories, Anne in *Ann of Green Gables* and, for the younger generation, probably any one of Jacqueline Wilson's creations. But as one of literature's functions is to help us get inside the heads of people perhaps very different from ourselves and extend the reach of our empathy, maybe we should grow beyond this and also give time to stories which offer insights into people more difficult to like or identify with.

> **TALKING POINTS** Which childhood literary heroes/heroines did you most identify with? Were there characters you enjoyed more than the ones you identified with? In your adult reading, which characters do you remember identifying with most strongly? Are there any books you've read at different times of your life and found

that your sympathies have shifted from one character to another? Are there any books you have loved despite the absence of characters you can easily identify with?

ILLUSTRATIONS IN NOVELS

There was a particular vogue for these in the nineteenth century, though in the eighteenth new editions of books already selling well might be enhanced by a few specially commissioned illustrations.

It was the illustrations in Dickens' novels – starting with *The Pickwick Papers* (1836), published in serialised form – that really started the trend. Booksellers often used the illustrations as window advertising.

The strong characterisation and vividly described locations, as well as the dramatic plot incidents, meant that Dickens' novels were particularly well suited to illustration, and there were a total of nine hundred to his novels.

Although book illustration wasn't lucrative, some artists used the work as a stepping-stone in their careers, while more established artists sometimes used it as a way of topping up their income.

With improvements in printing techniques towards the end of the nineteenth century, novels with high quality illustrations – especially by the Pre-Raphaelite artists – became popular for their illustrations rather than the text. But by the start of the twentieth century, few illustrated novels were published. It is generally thought that our visual interests were catered for by the use of photography and film.

Illustrations are now mainly confined to books for younger readers.

IMAGINATION

One of the faculties that divides human beings from the rest of creation. It is highly developed in writers of fiction who, through their work, help to develop it in their readers. Entering worlds other than our own, through reading, not only enriches us; it gives us some idea of what it might be like to be someone other than ourselves. And be able to imagine a world different from the one we know might encourage us to change our world for the better – or to take on board the warnings conveyed in some futuristic, science fiction novels … and avoid the predicted catastrophes. Could be useful.

IMPAC AWARD

Or, more correctly, the International IMPAC Dublin Literary Award. It's one of the richest literary prizes in the world, standing at 100,000 euros. Sponsored by the IMPAC company and administered by Dublin City Public Libraries, it's open to novels in any language by writers of any nationality – though the novel has to have been published in English or English translation. Unlike most other literary prizes, there's always a two-year lapse between date of publication and the year a novel becomes eligible for the award. Books are nominated by public libraries world-wide. It's recognised as the most eclectic and unpredictable of all literary awards and brings strange bedfellows together on the same nomination list. It has, however, picked out some future **Nobel Prize** winners – such as Turkish writer Orhan Pamuk who won the IMPAC with *My Name is Red* in 2003.

IMPRINT

The trade name under which a work is published. One company may have multiple imprints, used to market works to different groups of consumers, though sometimes a company's multiple imprints are the result of it having taken over smaller companies. The Penguin Group imprints, for example, include Allen Lane, Dorling Kindersley, Michael Joseph, Viking Press, Penguin Classics, Ladybird Books, and Puffin Books. The Random House company publishes the imprints Vintage, Chatto and Windus, Doubleday, Ballantine Books and others. And now that Penguin and Random House have merged to create the world's biggest publishing group, all these imprints (and a number of others) are under the auspices of one company.

INDEPENDENT BOOKSHOPS

Sadly, a dying breed, suffocated by a mixture of on-line book-buying, **e-books**, and the end of the **Net Book Agreement**, the latter enabling the big chains and supermarkets to sell books at greatly reduced prices because they buy in bulk at a discount. But there is nothing as pleasurable as spending time in a really good independent bookshop where the stock is hand-picked by a knowledgeable and dedicated bookseller with an eye for the interesting and 'different' and the knack of displaying books in such a way that, every time you go into the shop, your attention is caught by some new treasure. *Proper* bookshops. Support them whenever you can. Life will be the worse without them.

INDEPENDENT PUBLISHERS

Publishers not part of a group or large conglomerate. A few are sizeable and very successful companies – such as Bloomsbury and Faber. But many are much smaller and it is often these who bring out some of the most interesting new writing. In fact, the primacy of profit in much mainstream publishing has actually stimulated the founding of a number of small independent publishers that focus on particular aspects of the book market – such as translated writing (see the excellent little publishers And Other Stories and Peirene Press).

INDEX, THE

The list of books banned by the Catholic church between its instigation in 1559 and its formal abolition in 1966. As well as early scientific works challenging the accepted theological accounts of the world and the universe (including those by Galileo and Giordano Bruno – burnt at the stake for advocating Pantheism – and, later, Charles Darwin), the Index included the *Essays* of Montaigne (1533–92) and the works of Enlightenment thinkers of the eighteenth century (such as Voltaire and Diderot). Apart from books unacceptable on theological grounds, the Index included those judged to be a danger to morals and therefore banned works by a good many writers of fiction – attesting to the perceived power of fiction to influence our actions and the way we think. Here are just a few of the writers to find themselves and their works (sometimes individual works, sometime their whole *œuvre*) on the list: Daniel Defoe, Jonathan Swift, Samuel Richardson, Stendhal, Victor Hugo, Honoré de Balzac, Gustav Flaubert, André Gide, Graham Greene. And, unsurprisingly, the 'scurrilous' writings of Casanova and the Marquis de Sade were there, too.

> **TALKING POINT**   Is there ever a case to be made for banning a book?

INK

Wonderful stuff that we take for granted. The Chinese were already making it 23 centuries BCE, and it was widely used in ancient India. In ancient Greece and Rome ink was made from soot, glue and water, while Mediaeval Europe used a mixture of ferrous sulphate, gall, gum, and water. But this was no good for use with the printing press, and a new kind of ink had to be developed (from soot, turpentine, and walnut oil, apparently). Today, inks use a complicated mix of chemicals.

Civilisation as we know it would not be possible without ink … The same goes for paper.

INTERIOR MONOLOGUE

The direct representation of a character's thoughts, without the intervention of a narrator. Although resembling **stream-of-consciousness**, the interior monologue tends to follow a more organised line of thought and does not disrupt the thoughts with random perceptions of the outside world or half-formed associations (which is the case with stream-of-consciousness writing). It's an effective way of getting on the inside of a character and seeing things from their point of view.

INTERNATIONAL BOOK FAIRS

… are not for the faint-hearted, but can provide a fascinating insight into the book trade for those not directly involved in publishing. They are stimulating but exhausting junkets for publishers, agents, translators, writers and would-be writers who come together from all over the world to do deals (buying and selling 'rights'), flog their wares, learn about the latest publishing trends, listen to well-known writers speak, attend seminars, drum up business, and see friends. Members of the public can gain entry, usually at a price – although possibly the greatest Fair of them all, the Frankfurt International Book Fair, invites the public in on the final day. (The venue for the Frankfurt Fair is so vast that there is a constant parade of little buses ferrying attendees between the various buildings of the Fair's enormous site.)

Some fairs will invite a different country each year to be 'Guest of honour' or 'Market Focus', giving that country wonderful opportunities to inform the world about their writers and their publishing industry.

A number of the world's great cities host International Book Fairs – including London, Tokyo, Beijing, Cape Town, Hong Kong, Krakow, New Delhi and Istanbul, with Fairs specifically for children's publishing held in Shanghai and, most famously, Bologna. The biggest North American event, BookExpo America, is held in various cities across the continent.

If you're in London at the time of the Book Fair (usually April), it's worth a visit. And you can pick up some nice 'freebies' – including a very useful booky **tote bag** … or two.

ISBN

The unique International Standard Book Number assigned to every book published (apart from some self-published volumes) enables bookshops and libraries to order and track books and is therefore an important commercial tool. Originally a nine-digit number, then ten, it now comprises thirteen digits which encode basic information about the book, such as country, language, name of publisher, book title and type (the hardback will have a different number from the paperback, for example), ending with a 'check digit' which validates the preceding numbers. A book's ISBN is stated on the initial page of publication information (along with copyright notices etc) and appears on the back cover, too, where it is also represented in barcode format, allowing easy electronic recording. Each country has its own ISBN registration organisation and publishers have to pay for the purchase of ISBN numbers.

J

Emperor Julien – "Some love horses, others love wild animals; but I myself, since childhood, have been seized by an overwhelming desire to buy, to possess books."

JACKETS/COVERS

Strictly speaking, a book 'jacket' refers to the removable, wrap-around cover of the traditional hardback. But the term is often used interchangeably with 'cover' as they do more or less the same job.

'Never judge a jacket by its book' – that's the advice of American humourist Fran Lebowitz (author of the best-selling *Metropolitan Life*). And it's true that just occasionally we can be 'grabbed' by a really gorgeous cover … only to be disappointed by the book it's helping to sell – because, yes, one of the jobs the jacket has to do (apart from giving information – author's name, title, publisher, description, endorsements, book category, price, ISBN) is to arouse your interest sufficiently to make you *pick the book up*. It's said that a book cover has something like 1.5 seconds to make an impact on the eye when potential readers encounter a number of books displayed face out. 1.5 seconds. It's asking a lot.

In France, however, there's a tradition of more literary publications having very plain covers – just title, author, and publisher on the front in a simple font on a white or cream background. This very simplicity seems to be their mark of distinction – as if those books are above the usual hurly-burly of commercialism.

Fashions change in book jackets, as in everything else – as can easily be seen by comparing successive editions of a 'classic', for example. (Some are collected on-line.) And different publishing houses and imprints will sometimes adopt a 'house style' to make their books distinctive – the smart black of Penguin Classics, the particular green of those original **Virago** books, the distinctive beauty of books published by Persephone.

Cover designs differ hugely, but there is one 'truth' designers have to bear in mind: apparently, men never buy books with pink on the cover ...

TALKING POINTS/SOMETHING TO THINK ABOUT 1 Have you ever been led to buy a book because you liked the cover?

2 Do you have any books whose covers you feel perfectly fit the contents? – or any whose covers are 'misleading'?

> 3   Imagine the perfect cover for one of your favourite books …

JEWISH BOOK WEEK

One of the oldest book festivals in Britain, it began in 1952. Held in late February/early March, it's a nine-day celebration and exploration of Jewish thought, history, literature, and general culture, with particular attention to books published within the preceding year.

The festival invites guests from all over the world to engage with ideas and issues relevant to Jewish life, and attracts an international audience of both Jewish and non-Jewish visitors. Since 2012, the festival has been located at the new arts venue of King's Place – part of the recently regenerated King's Cross area of London.

JOIE DE VIVRE

The joy of living. Increased by reading. (If it's not, why bother?)

K

Franz Kafka – "A book must be the axe for the frozen sea within us."

KALIMA PROJECT

A visionary project to translate a vast array of the world's greatest books into Arabic. With a generous grant from the Abu Dhabi Authority for Culture and Heritage, plus the support of the Crown Prince of Abu Dhabi, it aims to make available much more of the world's cultural heritage to Arabic readers in their own beautiful and expressive language. It is the attempt to bridge the gap of a thousand years: in the first millennium CE – while Europe languished in its so-called 'Dark Ages' – it was Arabic scholars who led the world in producing, translating, and preserving knowledge in many fields. But for various historical, social and political reasons, this has not been the case in the second millennium.

As well as making the world's major texts available in Arabic, the Kalima Project aims to improve the mechanisms of book production, quality and distribution across the Arab world. The belief behind the project – that knowledge and books inspire intellectual and economic development, enrich lives, stimulate healthy debate and bridge cultural gaps – is one that some parts of the non-Arab world need reminding of … especially those in power who are busy decimating our libraries, as well as driving our publishing industry to become a purely profit-driven enterprise.

And in case you were wondering what that beautiful word 'Kalima' means, it's simply Arabic for 'word'.

KEEPING UP WITH THE (LITERARY) JONESES

… those people who manage to read the whole of the Booker short list within a fortnight of it being announced, who will agree with or refute all the opinions in the review pages of newspapers (because, yes, they've read those books, too), and who talk about 'going to **Hay**' – or Edinburgh or Cheltenham – rather as we might refer to popping out to Tesco's. *Don't let them bother you.* If you prefer to spend your time **re-reading** *Winnie-the-Pooh* or *Little Women* or *War and Peace*, then go ahead. The titles of the Booker shortlist will still be around next year and what's really worth reading will have floated to the surface. Reading is for pleasure; it's not another form of social competition. Leave those literary Joneses to it.

KINDLE

Verb   **1** to set alight or start to burn   **2** to arouse or be aroused   **3** to make or become bright.

Noun   Hand-held device designed and marketed by **Amazon** which allows you to download and read ebooks, magazines, newspapers, etc. The name was thought to be appropriate as a metaphor for 'intellectual excitement' associated with the word's implication of 'lighting a fire' (not, we hope, a fire on which to burn traditional books ...).

The Kindle and similar devices have revolutionised reading and book production. Down-loadable books – cheaper than hard copies – now account for a huge proportion of publishing sales. (See also **e-books**.)

L

D. H. Lawrence – "The novel is the highest form of human expression so far attained."

LEGAL DEPOSIT LIBRARIES

Every UK publisher, big or small, has the obligation to send one copy of every book published to our six Legal Deposit Libraries. These are: the British Library (London); the National Library of Scotland; the Bodleian Library (Oxford); the Cambridge University Library; Trinity College Library (Dublin); and the National Library of Wales (Aberystwyth).

These libraries are alerted to the publication of books through the registering of their ISBN numbers. Publishers are sent requests for copies by the British Library and also by the ALDL (Agency for the Legal Deposit Libraries) which acts on behalf of the other five. The books are then available for users of those libraries to order from the well-named 'stacks'. It's a good idea, and a bit like the great **Library of Alexandria**.

LIBRARIAN(S)

Remember that quiet girl in your class at school? – the one with the glasses and her nose always in a book? – not top of the class, but definitely not at the bottom. She could always be relied on to be helpful … So no-one was surprised when she became a librarian.

That's the stereotype, of course, and most of us have known some pretty lively, outgoing librarians. But the professional librarians – highly qualified, widely read – that used to man your local library are becoming a rare breed … in fact, an endangered species as those 'unavoidable cutbacks' in library services cull the top ranking (and therefore more expensive) librarians and rely increasingly on library assistants to run the show. These do a magnificent job, keeping the show on the road. But diminishing the role of the highly qualified librarian downgrades the whole sense of what libraries stand for.

There are posts available to those 'culled' librarians in university and specialist libraries, but with so many professional librarians applying, the competition is likely to be greater than it's ever been.

But anyone who works in a library – whether highly qualified or a volunteer – can relish being part of a long, long history of librarianship. Librarians have helped to shape cultures, history, and many great human beings.

The history of librarianship goes right back at least to Ashurbanipal, the eighth-century BCE King of Assyria. He founded a library in his palace at Nineveh (in Mesopotamia) and employed someone to organise and look after the thousands of tablets on which information and literary texts were inscribed.

The great **Library of Alexandria** counted the famous dramatist Aristophanes among its many prestigious librarians.

The monasteries of the Middle Ages housed the most important libraries of Europe and were originally overseen by the monk in charge of book copying (an important monastic activity), though this function gradually developed into the more demanding job of proper classification and cata-loguing. And by the fourteenth century, universities were also employing librarians.

With the explosion of enthusiasm for learning that characterised the Renaissance, the role of libraries in the lives of both wealthy individuals and a wider public steadily increased, with the accompanying growth in the role of the librarian. Two important figures in the history of British librarianship are John Dury (1596-1680) and Sir Thomas Bodley (1545-1613). In 1650, Dury published *The Reformed Librarie-keeper*, detailing the duties and functions of professional librarians, advising that they should be well-educated and thus able to maintain high standards in the stewardship of their libraries. And it was Bodley who established Oxford's great Bodleian Library in 1602.

In France, as a result of the Revolution of 1789, librarians became responsible for selecting books suitable for all 'citizens', regardless of wealth and education – which can be seen as the beginnings of a modern public library service.

With the growing complexities and extent of libraries, formal qualifications in librarianship came into being. (Melvil Dewey – of the **Dewey Decimal System** – founded the first American school for library science at Columbia University in 1887.) The original Batgirl character was given a doctorate in Library Science and employed as the head of Gotham City Public Library.

With the coming of the digital age, librarians no longer simply deal with books, of course – though they still have to spend part of their working day putting books on shelves … in the right places.

Some famous people who, at some point in their lives, were librarians:

David Hume (1711–1776) – Scottish philosopher

Casanova (1725–1798) – Yes, really! (Later in life he became librarian to the Count of Waldstein in Bohemia)

Lewis Carroll (1832–1898) – author

Marcel Duchamps (1887–1968) – Dadaist artist

Mao Zedong (1893–1976) – leader of the Chinese Communist revolution (while working as an Assistant Librarian at Peking University, he was converted to Communism by the Marxist Chief Librarian).

J. Edgar Hoover (1895–1972) – first director of the FBI

Golda Meir (1898–1978) – fourth Prime Minister of Israel.

Jorge Luis Borges (1899–1986) – Argentinian writer

Philip Larkin (1922–1985) – English poet

LIBRARIES

Between cathedrals of culture and enlightenment and shabby swap-shops, libraries come in all shapes, sizes, and levels of excellence. But many a humble little library has made a genius out of a down-at-heel local child. Great or humble, ancient or modern, defend them with the last drop of your readerly blood.

LIBRARIES ARE ...

cathedrals of the mind
hospitals for the failing human spirit
clubs for the lonely
fair-grounds for the imagination
islands of thought in oceans of commercialism
escape routes from poverty and cultural limitation
a warm place on a cold day

something free in a world that increasingly defines value by wealth

And a nice quote from Jean Grenier (a French writer and teacher who befriended and encouraged the young Albert Camus): 'Like museums, libraries are a refuge from ageing, illness, and death.'

LIBRARIES IN FICTION

The most famous include

Jorge Luis Borges, 'The Library of Babel' (1941) – his famous short story of the universe as interlocking, book-lined hexagons … (said to be inspired by the 1901 short story by German writer Kurd Lasswitz, 'The Universal Library').

Elias Canetti, *Auto da Fé* (1935) The story of Peter Kien, a loner whose personal library means everything to him. It's one of the great, substantial works of pre-war European literature from a writer who was awarded the Nobel Prize in 1981.

Umberto Eco, *The Name of the Rose* (1980) A bestseller despite being Eco's first novel, it's a sophisticated medieval murder mystery set in a great abbey famous for its library. (Sean Connery starred in the film of the novel.)

Boris Pasternak, *Dr Zhivago* (1957) It's in a local library, where she works, that Yuri Zhivago re-encounters Larissa Antipova ('Lara') – with whom he'd previously worked in a field hospital. It marks the beginning of their affair which is the dominating relationship of the novel.

Jean-Paul Sartre, *Nausea* (1938) It's in the library of Bouville ('Mudtown') that the Autodidact – so despised by the protagonist Roquentin – is trying to educate himself by reading his way alphabetically through all the books on the shelves.

LIFE-WRITING

Closely allied to **autobiography** and **memoir**, but has a different nuance in its usage. Whereas the latter – particularly autobiography – are usually written by someone well-known in their field and in whose life many people will therefore be interested, 'life-writing' can be undertaken by anyone and is often a feature of creative writing courses. In some cases, the non-famous have interesting stories to tell, illuminating life in a particular time or place or social situation in the process of recounting their personal experiences. And some use it therapeutically to explore and express difficulties endured at certain periods of their lives. Some life-writing finds its way into print; much does not, but is nonetheless a valuable exercise for the writer. At its worst, it can descend into the indulgence of extreme individualism; at its best, it can give the reader access to a range of experiences and emotions that might not be encountered elsewhere.

LIPOGRAM

A work of literature in which the writer will impose a particular 'constraint' upon its composition – the avoidance of a particular letter, or certain letters. There are examples of lipograms from Ancient Greece, but the practice didn't really get off the ground until the twentieth century – and even then, examples are quite rare. There are, however, a couple of particularly famous ones worth knowing about.

The most famous example is the 1969 novel, *La Disparition*, by French writer and crossword composer Georges Perec. It's written entirely without the letter 'e'. Imagine – a French novel without a single 'le', for a start! But the 'e' exclusion is more than a word game: it holds symbolic significance linked to the 'disappearance' in the story ('La disparition', in French, can indicate a death as well as a disappearance) and is said to be linked to the 'disappearance' of both Perec's Jewish parents during the Second World War (his father in action, his mother in Auschwitz: he was cared for by relatives). This profound personal absence – symbolised by the letter vital to the language – also embodies the wider disappearance from European life of the millions of people who had contributed so much not just to French culture but to that of the continent as whole. Almost as remarkable as Perec's achievement was that of his translator, Gilbert Adair, who gave us the remarkable English version of the novel, *A Void* – again, entirely without the letter 'e' (so no 'the', 'he', 'she', 'here', 'there', 'where', 'when' …). The Spanish translator banned the letter 'a' from the novel – the equivalent, in terms of frequency and centrality in that language.

As if to compensate the banned 'e' of *La Disparition*, Perec went on to give it a novella all to itself, *Les Revenentes* (1972) – which means 'the ghosts', those that return … though, strictly speaking, it should be spelt '*revenantes*'. This was translated by Ian Monk as *The Exeter Text: Jewels, Secrets, Sex*.

The inspiration for Perec's novel came from a 1939 novel by American Ernest Vincent Wright, *Gadsby*, to which Perec was introduced by a member of the OULIPO group to which he belonged. This was also written without 'e'. It took Wright a number of years to complete, couldn't find a publisher, was eventually self-published, but most copies were destroyed in a warehouse fire. Wright died the same year. As a tribute to Wright, Perec included, in *La Disparition*, a character called Lord Gadsby V. Wright.

Another interesting variation on the lipogram is *Alphabetical Africa* (1974) by the Austrian-American writer Walter Abish. The first chapter is made up entirely of words beginning with 'a'; the second chapter allows words starting with both 'a' and 'b'; the third, 'a', 'b', 'c' … and so on. By chapter 26, anything goes. But then he reverses the process so the very last chapter again only uses 'a' words. A somewhat bizarre experiment, by writer and broadcaster Gyles Brandreth, was the rewriting of certain of Shakespeare's plays banning significant letters – such as 'i' from *Hamlet*, so that whether to be or not be becomes a 'query' rather than a 'question'.

SUGGESTED ACTIVITY   Try writing an e-less paragraph or two …

LITERARY AGENTS

… are the doctors' receptionists of the literary world: it sometimes seems to writers that literary agents are there to stop them getting at the publishers. These days, it's very hard for a writer to get publishers to read their work unless it has been submitted to them by a reputable literary agent – who will, if the book is accepted, take a cut (usually 10–15%) of whatever money the author receives.

With the restructuring of the publishing industry

in recent years, many traditional editors have been made redundant and certain aspects of their jobs taken over by literary agents who are expected to submit only books that are more or less ready for publication. At one time, editors would work with a promising author or book to turn it into a publishable one. Literary agents themselves are increasingly looking for books that will need little or no work in order to be published. This situation has spawned a host of **editing agencies** who, for a fee, will help authors work on their books to make them (possibly) more acceptable to agents ... and ultimately, publishers. (Hard luck if you can't afford it.)

LITERARY FAN CLUBS

Fans of pop idols and film stars have their 'fan clubs', so why shouldn't literature enthusiasts have the opportunity to mix with other members of their tribe? A good number of our most famous writers have societies dedicated to the enjoyment and promotion of their work. As well as holding events and conferences, they will usually provide information about the life and works of the author the society is dedicated to. But unlike 'Star Wars' conventions and similar events, one is not usually expected to 'dress up' – happily for us shy, retiring literary types. There's plenty of information on the web about these organisations, but here are a few to be going on with: the Jane Austen Society (in Britain) can be found at www.janeaustensoci.freeuk.com, though there are further groups in other parts of the world. The Dickens Fellowship, founded in 1902, is worldwide and can be found on www.thedickensfellowship.org. And of course there's the Bard's fan club on shakespearesociety.org, and lots of local ones too. The Virginia Woolf Society is very good (www.virginiawoolfsociety.co.uk) and enthusiasts for George Orwell have the Orwell Society (www.orwellsociety.com).

LITERARY FICTION

Sometimes – especially in the past – referred to as 'quality fiction', a term no longer favoured in the modern democracy of literature. Literary fiction does not fit into – nor is it marketed as – any of the recognised genres, although it may use features familiar from certain genres. One example would be Margaret Atwood's *The Handmaid's Tale* (1985) which is set in an imagined future and so shares elements of **science fiction**.

Books categorised as 'literary fiction' have a depth, complexity, and individuality usually absent from genre fiction, while their considered and usually more sophisticated use of language further differentiate them from most genre fiction. Some high quality genre fiction may be shelved, in bookshops, under both categories – 'Genre' and 'Literary' or 'General Fiction'. But not all books in the 'General Fiction' section will be what most people mean by 'literary fiction'.

> **TALKING POINT** What, for you, are the qualities that would place a book in the category of 'literary fiction'? What examples come most readily to mind?

LITERARY REVIEW

A lively and intelligent magazine for people who love reading but don't like 'intellectual jargon'. It was founded in 1979 by Dr Anne Smith of Edinburgh University's English Department. Since 1993, it has also been known for giving the annual **'Bad Sex in Fiction' award** for the worst description of a sex scene in literature.

LITERATURE ENGAGÉE

Fiction written out of commitment, to strongly promote a particular (usually political) agenda. The fact that we've adopted the elegant French term (in preference to the rather ugly English translation, 'engaged literature') alerts one to the fact that the French proved particularly good at it. It became popular just after the Second World War when French Existentialists – and Jean-Paul Sartre in particular – revived the idea of the artist's serious responsibility to society. Sartre's *Roads to Freedom* trilogy is a good example of *literature engagée.*

LITTLE MAGAZINES

Literary magazines produced without regard for monetary gain but with the aim of introducing new authors – and often new ways of writing – to their (often quite small number of) readers. Many an established author has had their first publication in a 'little magazine', and the dedication of those who produce them should be acknowledged and celebrated. Some last for only a few issues or appear sporadically, some manage to keep going for years and come out regularly. They are too numerous to mention by name, but both the **British Library** and the **Poetry Library** hold substantial collections of them.

LONDON REVIEW OF BOOKS, THE

Founded in 1979, during the year-long lock-out at the *Times*, the LRB (as it is affectionately known) has stood up for the tradition of 'the literary and intellectual essay in English'. With two issues each month, it contains up to fifteen essay-length reviews by academics, journalists and writers, along with shorter pieces on art and films, as well as poems and a letters page.

Always aiming to combine '*topicality with depth and scholarship with good writing*', it isn't afraid to challenge received ideas – perhaps one of the reasons it has the largest circulation of any literary magazine in Europe. It has an unmatched international reputation and is an 'institution' British book-lovers can be well and truly proud of (even if you don't read it). And the front cover illustrations are delightful …

LONDON REVIEW OF BOOKS BOOKSHOP, THE

It opened in 2003. Go there if you can. It's in a little side street just opposite the British Museum in the Bloomsbury district of London. It isn't particularly big (though bigger than it looks – there's quite a large basement), but the stock is wonderfully chosen and displayed in such a way as to draw attention to interesting new titles you might otherwise have missed – as well as some mainstream favourites. And the staff are very well-informed and helpful.

It's also got a lovely little café which is very popular (hard to get a seat sometimes!). It's the kind of excellent independent bookshop that needs our support if we are not to lose these precious gems of civilisation. The shop also hosts events with a wide range of interesting authors.

LONG BOOKS

'One always tends to overpraise a long book because one has got through it.' E. M. Forster, *Abinger Harvest*. But, let's face it, there are quite a few long books that deserve the praise. Here are a few long novels that come to mind (though not many people can claim to have read them all, so don't panic …):

Don Quixote, Miguel de Cervantes

Tom Jones, Henry Fielding

Clarissa, Samuel Richardson

War and Peace, Leo Tolstoy

The Brothers Karamazov, Fyodor Dostoyevsky

Moby Dick, Herman Melville

In Search of Lost Time, Marcel Proust

Petersburg, André Bely

The Magic Mountain, Thomas Mann

The Man Without Qualities, Robert Musil

Ulysses, James Joyce

Istanbul was a Fairy Tale, Mario Levi

LUNATICS

'Lunatics engage in imaginary dialogues which they hear echoing somewhere in their minds; readers engage in a similar dialogue provoked silently by words on a page.' Alberto Manguel, *A Reading Diary: A Year of Favourite Books* (2004)

M

André Maurois – "The art of reading is in great part that of acquiring a better understanding of life from one's encounter with it in a book."

MADELEINE

The most famous cake in literature. It's one of those soft little French cakes, the taste of which, dipped in tea, unlocks vivid memories of the past for Marcel in Proust's *In Search of Lost Time*. Here's part of the famous passage:

… one day in winter, when I came home, my mother, noticing I was cold, offered me some tea, a thing I did not normally take. I declined at first and then, for no special reason, changed my mind. She sent out for one of those small, plump little cakes known as *petites madeleines*, which look as though they've been moulded in the fluted scallop of a pilgrim's shell. […] I raised to my lips a spoonful of the tea in which I had soaked a morsel of the cake. No sooner had the warm liquid, and the crumbs with it, touched my palate than a shiver ran through my entire body and I stopped, intent upon the extraordinary changes taking place […] And suddenly the memory returned. The taste was that of the little crumb of madeleine which, on Sundays mornings at Combray (because on those mornings I didn't leave the house before it was time for church), when I went to say goodbye to her in her bedroom, my aunt Léonie used to give me, dipping it first in her own cup of real or lime-flower tea. […] And once I had recognised the taste of the crumb of madeleine soaked in the infusion of lime-flowers which my aunt used to give me (although I did not yet know and must long put off the discovery of why this memory made me so happy) immediately the old grey house, upon the street where her room was, rose up like the scenery in a theatre […] and along with the house the town as it was from morning to night and in all weathers – the Square where I was sent before lunch, the streets along which I used to run errands, the country roads where we walked when the weather was fine.

MAGIC REALISM

Or 'Magical Realism'. Fiction that incorporates fantastic or mythical elements into realistic settings and situations. It conveys a sense of the ordinary being miraculous and the miraculous as ordinary. Originally it was used of novels by a number of Latin American authors – particularly Gabriel Garcia Marquez (1927-2014) – but has more recently been used in a less precise way as a marketing tool for books containing any 'fantastic' element. True Magical Realism can be an effective way of exploring the experiences and world-views of people and communities outside what we think of as main-stream culture.

A few suggestions for some Magic Realist writers and novels to try, if you don't know them already:

Gabriel Garcia Marquez (1927–2014 Columbia): *One Hundred Years of Solitude* (1967)

Isabel Allende (b.1942 Chile): *House of Spirits* (1982)

Laura Esquivel (b.1950 Mexico): *Like Water for Chocolate* (1989)

Toni Morrison (b.1931 America): *Beloved* (1987)

Salman Rushdie (b.1947 India): *Midnight's Children* (1981)

Angela Carter (1940–1992 UK): *Nights at the Circus* (1984)

Ben Okri (b.1959 Nigeria): *The Famished Road* (1991)

MAN BOOKER PRIZE

Originally known as the **Booker-McConnell Prize** (after the company Booker-McConnell began sponsoring the event in 1968), it became known as the "Booker Prize" or simply "the Booker." When administration of the prize was transferred to the Booker Prize Foundation in 2002, the sponsor became the Man Group, which chose to retain "Booker" as part of the title of the prize. It's awarded each year for the best original novel, written in English.

Until 2014 the author had to be a citizen of the Commonwealth, the Republic of Ireland, or Zimbabwe, but the prize is now open to authors from anywhere in the world (though the work has to be in English and published in the UK). With prize money running at £50,000, it's one of the world's most generous literary prizes.

There have been a number of controversies surrounding the awarding of the prize, one of the most famous occurring in 1972 when winner John Berger protested, during his acceptance speech, against Booker McConnell, blaming Booker's 130 years of sugar production in the Caribbean for modern poverty in the region. (Berger donated half of his prize money to the British Black Panther movement.)

In 1980, Anthony Burgess refused to attend the ceremony unless it was confirmed in advance that he'd won. His was one of two books likely to win, the other being by William Golding. The judges decided only 30 minutes before the ceremony, giving the prize to Golding. And in 1983 a draw between J. M. Coetzee and Salman Rushdie left chair of judges Fay Weldon to choose between them. Apparently she chose Rushdie, only to change her mind as the result was being phoned through.

In September 2013 it was announced that future Man Booker Prize awards would consider authors from anywhere in the world, causing controversy in the literary world.

The advisory committee for the Booker includes a writer, two publishers, a literary agent, a bookseller, a librarian, and a chairperson appointed by the Booker

Prize Foundation. This committee selects the judging panel from amongst leading literary critics, writers, academics and leading public figures. The winner is announced at a ceremony in London's Guildhall, usually in early October.

To mark the 25th anniversary of the prize, in 1993, it was decided to choose a *Booker of Bookers Prize* – which went to Salman Rushdie's *Midnight's Children*. The same book won the 'Best of the Booker' in 2008 (celebrating 40 years of the prize), based on a public vote.

Twenty-first century winners of the prize are

2000   Margaret Atwood, *The Blind Assassin*

2001   Peter Carey, *True History of the Kelly Gang*

2002   Yann Martel, *Life of Pi*

2003   D.B.C. Pierre, *Vernon God Little*

2004   Alan Holinghurst, *The Line of Beauty*

2005   John Banville, *The Sea*

2006   Kiran Desai, *The Inheritance of Loss*

2007   Anne Enright, *The Gathering*

2008   Aravind Adiga, *The White Tiger*

2009   Hilary Mantel, *Wolf Hall*

2010   Howard Jacobson, *The Finkler Question*

2011   Julian Barnes, *The Sense of an Ending*

2012   Hilary Mantel, *Bring Up the Bodies*

2013   Eleanor Catton, *The Luminaries*

> **TALKING POINT** Do you approve of the decision to open the Man Booker Prize to writers from all over the world? What differences do you think it will make to the prize?

MANGA

Originally comics created in Japan, Manga are now popular world-wide. Though regarded as a contemporary publishing phenomenon worth billions of pounds, they have their roots in the long history of Japanese art. However, there is also evidence that US comics and Disney animated films – taken to Japan by the occupying American forces after World War II – have had some influence on its development.

A broad range of genres can be found in the Manga format and they are a major part of the Japanese publishing industry. They are close relatives of the **graphic novel** and *bande desinée* – which itself has developed a sub-genre known as '*la nouvelle manga*', imitating the illustrative style of Japanese Manga. The vigorous, expressive style of Manga illustrations makes the form particularly popular with the young.

MARY MAGDALENE

… is often depicted as reading a book in paintings by the Old Masters. (So you're in good company.)

MASH-UP NOVEL

… or 'mashup' or 'mashed-up novel'. A hybrid (as in its use in the music industry) that combines an existing work of literature – usually a well-known classic – with another genre, showing a particular *penchant* for vampires, werewolves and zombies. Examples are *Pride and Prejudice and Zombies* and, yes, *Sense and Sensibility and Seamonsters*. Possibly not for the faint-hearted … or true lovers of Literature with a capital L … But all right for a bit of fun, we suppose.

MEDICAL ROMANCE

(See DOCTOR/NURSE ROMANCE)

MEMOIR

Related to biography and autobiography, but whereas these usually deal with the whole of the subject's life (or their life so far, if still alive), a 'memoir' usually deals with a particular portion or aspect of a person's life, and is often quite short. The writer of the memoir may be writing primarily about themselves or maybe recalling memories of a famous person they happen to have known at a particular period of their life.

MILLS AND BOON

… started life as a general publisher, founded in 1908 by Gerald Rusgrove Mills and Charles Boon, but began to specialise in escapist romantic fiction for women in the 1930s when the Depression made such stories popular as a welcome escape from the hard realities of daily life. Often dismissed as low-brow, simple in style and formulaic, the pleasure they bring to their many, many readers cannot be denied and their predictability in terms of relationships and happy endings are part of the reason for their success.

Originally published as hardbacks and distributed through lending libraries, the 1950s saw a move towards the production of cheap, affordable paperbacks available through newsagents. Operating through a combination of retail and subscription sales, Mills and Boon titles are said to have over 3,000,000 readers annually in the UK alone (and there are plenty of others worldwide). The advent of ebooks has benefitted the imprint greatly: they release more than a hundred each month which now outsell their physical books.

Critics of the imprint accuse the books of perpetuating the submission of women and even playing into the hands of rape fantasies, encouraging unhealthy and old-fashioned models of relationships between the sexes. This was certainly true of the older books, but some more recent strands of the brand have stronger, more active female protagonists and a more up-to-date representation of sexual relationships.

TALKING POINT   Can reading Mills and Boon-type stories create unreal or harmful relationship models that lead to unhappiness in women's lives? – or should they just be seen as 'a little holiday from life'?

MISERY MEMOIRS

Also known as 'miserylit' (or 'mislit'), 'mismems' or even 'misery porn', this genre details the sufferings of the protagonist (usually telling the 'story' themselves) in childhood and their eventual triumph over adversity. The publication, in 1995, of American Dave Peltzer's memoir, *A Child Called It*, marks the launch of the genre (though it has been suggested that books like *Oliver Twist* are early fictional examples of this type of writing). In 1996, Irish writer Frank McCourt's *Angela's Ashes* (detailing his difficult, poverty-stricken childhood in New York and Ireland) increased the vogue for such writing. A huge number of books purporting to be stories of childhood abuse and suffering followed on from these as publishers rushed to satisfy a public appetite for this type of narrative – though a number of them have proved to be fiction rather than true memoirs, as claimed.

Some bookshops even have dedicated sections for 'Painful Lives' or 'Tragic Life Stories', though most sales of such books are now through supermarkets, and the readership is almost entirely female.

TALKING POINT Does the appeal of the genre depend on (1) an unhealthy voyeurism on the part of the reader? (2) a new willingness to confront difficult topics, such as child abuse? (3) the help it can give readers to come to terms with their own difficult pasts?

MURDER MYSTERY

See **Crime Fiction**

N

Charles Nodier – "Next to the pleasure of owning books, there is scarcely anything more pleasurable than talking about them."

NATIONAL BOOK AWARDS

See **'Nibbies'**

'NEITHER A BORROWER NOR A LENDER BE'

'Neither a borrower nor a lender be,
For loan oft loses both itself and friend,
And borrowing dulls the edge of husbandry.'

William Shakespeare

Some would say that if a book is worth reading, it's worth buying.

Some wouldn't. (Some can't afford it.)

NET BOOK AGREEMENT (or NBA)

An agreement between booksellers and publishers setting the price at which books were to be sold. It came into effect on the first day of the twentieth century, and publishers would refuse to supply any bookseller not complying with the agreement.

The agreement did not cover damaged books, however, and some stores deliberately damaged stock (often staining the edges of pages with a marker pen) so that they could sell them off more cheaply – especially if the books were not selling well.

The Restrictive Practices Court, which had looked at the NBA in 1962 and decided it was in the best interests of publishing to keep the agreement (best-sellers helped to fund worthwhile but less widely read authors), reviewed the agreement again in 1994, and by 1997 – after bitter struggles and campaigning within the book industry – decided that the NBA was not in the public interest.

The winners from this ruling were the big book chains and the supermarkets who could buy in bulk and offer books at knock-down prices – as well as the readers of the kind of books offered at low prices. The losers were the small, independent book-shops and countless authors whose work publishers could no longer fund because of reduced profits on best-sellers.

'NIBBIES'

These awards have been called 'the Oscars of British books'. The nickname, 'Nibbies', comes from the golden nib-shaped trophy given to winners. Launched in 1990, the prizes were originally known as the British Book Awards and were promoted by *Publishing News* (the book trade magazine). In 2010 and 2011, they became the Galaxy National Book Awards, then, in 2012, with sponsorship from the optician chain 'Specsavers', they became the Specsavers National Book Awards – though often referred to simply as the National Book Awards.

The awards are not just 'literary': they cover most publishing genres and relate to the general contribution of the author to the publishing industry as a whole. Winners are chosen by an 'Academy' drawn from many parts of the industry.

To give an idea of the scope of the prizes, the award of 'Author of the Year' has been given to, among others, the Prince of Wales (1990), Salman Rushdie (1996), Nigella Lawson (2001), Sheila Hancock (2005), and Hilary Mantel (2010 and 2012).

The 'Outstanding Achievement' award (until 2009 the 'Lifetime Achievement' award) has been given to writers as different as Delia Smith (1995), Jilly Cooper (1998), Spike Milligan (2000), Alan Bennett (2003), Sir David Attenborough (2004), Jamie Oliver (2006); J. K. Rowling (2008), and Jackie Collins (2011).

'Book of the Year' awards have gone from Yung Chang's *Wild Swans* (1994) to *Fifty Shades of Grey* (2012) by way of *The Da Vinci Code* (2003).

Prize categories have expanded during the awards' history, and sometimes 'shift'. Apart from those mentioned above, there are, for example, prizes in Popular Fiction, Popular Non-Fiction, Biography/ Autobiography, Crime Thrillers, Food and Drink, Children's, International Author of the Year and Audiobooks.

NOBEL PRIZE FOR LITERATURE

One of the five prizes awarded annually (winner announced in October) thanks to the bequest of Swedish arms manufacturer and inventor of dynamite Alfred Nobel (1833–96). He made the bequest after reading his own obituary – printed in error when it was in fact his brother who had died – which criticised him as a 'merchant of death'. Wanting to be remembered more positively, he used his accumulated fortune to finance prizes in Physics, Chemistry, Physiology/Medicine, Literature, and Peace.

The first Nobel Prize for Literature was awarded in 1901 to the French poet and essayist, Sully Prudhomme. According to the terms of Nobel's will, the winner of the Literature prize should, in their work, demonstrate 'idealism' as well as literary excellence – which possibly accounts for the fact that James Joyce was not among those receiving the prize. Still the most prestigious and wealthy prize, it has not been without controversy. The 'idealism' element tends, these days, to be connected specifically with Human Rights issues and has led to a more political slant to the awarding of the prize which – as well as a large sum of money – presents the winner with a gold medal and a personalised citation, at the annual ceremony in Stockholm. The highlight of the ceremony is usually the speech made by the Nobel Laureate.

A selection of Nobel Laureates ... (with those writing in English highlighted):

1907 Rudyard Kipling; 1913 Rabindranath Tagore; 1920 Knut Hamsun 1921 Anatole France; **1923 W. B. Yeats**; **1925 George Bernard Shaw;** 1929 Thomas Mann; **1930 Sinclair Lewis**; **1932 John Gallsworthy**; 1934 Luigi Pirandello; **1936 Eugene O'Neil**; **1938 Pearl S. Buck**; 1945 Gabriella Mistral; 1946 Herman Hesse; 1947 André Gide; **1948 T. S. Eliot**; **1949 William Faulkner**; **1950 Bertrand Russell**; 1952 François Mauriac; **1953 Winston Churchill**; **1954 Ernest Hemingway;** 1957 Albert Camus; 1958 Boris Pasternak; **1962 John Steinbeck**; 1964 Jean-Paul Sartre (who declined it); 1965 Mikhail Sholokov; **1969 Samuel Beckett**; 1970 Alexander Solzhenitsyn; 1971 Pablo Neruda; 1972 Heinrick Böll; **1973 Patrick White**; **1976 Saul Bellow**; 1980 Czesław Miłosz; 1981 Elias Canetti; 1982 Gabriel Garcia Marquez; **1983 William Golding**; 1985 Claude Simon; **1986 Wole Soyinka**; 1988 Naguib Mahfouz; 1990 Octavio Paz; **1991 Nadine Gordimer**; **1992 Derek Walcott**; **1993 Toni Morrison**; **1995 Seamus Heaney**; 1997 Dario Fo; 1998 José Saramago; 1999 Günter Grass; 2000 Gao Xingjian; **2001 V. S. Naipaul**; **2003 J. M.**

Coetzee; **2005 Harold Pinter**; 2006 Orhan Pamuk; **2007 Doris Lessing**; 2008 J. M. G. Le Clézio; 2009 Herta Müller; 2010 Mario Vargas Llosa; 2011 Tomas Tranströer; 2012 Mo Yan; **2013 Alice Munro.**

NOIR FICTION

Noir: French for 'black' – so not exactly full of light, colour and joy. It's rather like the genre known as **hardboiled**, though in 'noir' fiction the protagonist tends to be a victim, suspect, or criminal rather than a detective, though not always. Closely related to 'film noir', two well-known practitioners of the genre are James Elroy and Patricia Highsmith.
(See also **Scandinavian Noir**.)

NOM DE PLUME

Literally 'pen name' – the French word for pen coming from the original feather quill that pens used to be. Some authors choose to give themselves a 'writing name': the most famous include George Orwell, who was really called Eric Blair (which, it's true, lacks 'gravitas'); George Eliot was born Mary Ann Evans but adopted a man's name in order to be taken seriously at a time when 'lady novelists' were not (the George was from her beloved George Henry Lewes, with whom she 'lived in sin', defying the repressive morality of the time); for their early publications, the three Brontë sisters adopted names which would not give away their gender but were not obviously masculine, choosing names that preserved their initials – Charlotte became 'Currer', Emily became Ellis, and Ann became Acton, and they all took the surname Bell.

NON-FICTION

Obviously, any book that's not fiction. But the dividing line between the two is not always as clear-cut as one imagines. In history, biography and auto-biography, for example, the narrative is shaped by a particular consciousness making particular choices, writing from a certain point of view, deciding what to put in and what to leave out and how to colour events. A history of the Iraq War, for example, is likely to be written very differently from an American and Iraqi point of view.

> **TALKING POINT**   It's a frequently observed phenomenon that, as readers age, they tend to turn more towards non-fiction. Does anyone know why?

NORDIC NOIR (See **Scandinavian Noir**)

NOVEL, A (VERY) BRIEF HISTORY OF THE

Even in Classical times there were novels – we have a few complete and a number of fragments. Then the Mediaeval period gave us 'romances' – stories of knights and heroes – plus the less lofty tales and exempla popular among the less educated. Elements of the mediaeval romance continued into the Renaissance, the first landmarks of the period, in terms of prose fiction, being *Arcadia* by Sir Philip Sidney (1554–1586) and Lyly's *Euphues* (1578). Pilgrim in John Bunyan's *The Pilgrim's Progress* (1678 and second part 1684) wanders through the world somewhat like a knight errant of Mediaeval literature, while stories of such knights are what inspire Cervantes' self-styled Don Quixote de la Mancha to go out into the world with the purpose of righting wrongs – leading to a series of hilarious adventures and the making of the first great novel of the kind we recognise as such today.

But it isn't until the eighteenth century that the novel as we know it really gets going, with such narratives as **Daniel Defoe**'s *The Life and Strange Surprising Adventures of Robinson Crusoe* (1719), and his subsequent novels – *Captain Singleton* (1720), *Moll Flanders*, *A Journal of the Plague Year* and *Colonel Jack* (all 1722), and *Roxana* (1724) – **picaresque** in manner, rather than having tightly constructed plots. For that we have to wait until **Samuel Richardson** (1689–1761) published his **epistolary novel** *Pamela* in 1740, the success of which encouraged him to write *Clarissa*, appearing in eight volumes between

1747 and 1748, and then *Sir Charles Grandison* (1753–1754).

Partly in response to what he saw as the sentimentality and shallow ethics of Richardson's novels, **Henry Fielding** (1707–1754) set out to write more rollicking, full-blooded but compassionate narratives such as *Joseph Andrews* (1742) and the still much-loved *Tom Jones* (1749). Although the name of **Tobias Smollett** (1721–1771) is often associated with that of Henry Fielding, Smollett lacked the broad and attractive humanity of Fielding and, as a result, is less read today than Fielding.

Ten years after *Tom Jones* come the first two volumes of the still much loved *Life and Adventures of Tristram Shandy* (1759) by clergyman **Laurence Sterne** (1713–1768). The humour, playfulness and broad humanity of the work have endeared it to modern readers and it still receives a great deal of critical attention.

Towards the end of the eighteenth century, **Fanny Burney** (1752–1840) broke the male dominance of the novel with *Evelina* (1778) and *Cecilia* (1782) and though these were popular at the time, it is her diary, reflecting the life of the period, that has remained her most lasting literary legacy.

Also beginning to appear (coinciding with the emergence of the Romantic Movement) were **Gothic**

novels such as *The Castle of Otranto* (1764) by **Horace Walpole** and, somewhat later, *The Mysteries of Udolpho* (1794) by **Anne Radcliffe**. And it's as we move into the nineteenth century that the truly great era of the British novel begins, encouraged by a rapidly growing readership, made up increasingly of women.

The novels of **Maria Edgeworth** (1767–1849) harness the novel to a social purpose, painting contemporary society and pointing out some of its ills. However, it was **Jane Austen** (1775–1817), focusing on a narrower social range, that is recognised as the first great writer of the mature novel form with *Sense and Sensibility* (1811), *Pride and Prejudice* (1813), *Mansfield Park* (1814), *Emma* (1815), and the posthumously published *Northanger Abbey* and *Persuasion*. In paying tribute to her, the historical novelist **Sir Walter Scott** (1771–1832) said: *'That young lady had a talent for describing the involvements, feelings, and characters of ordinary life which is to me the most wonderful I have ever met with. The big bow-wow I can do myself like anyone going, but the exquisite touch which renders commonplace things and characters interesting from the truth of the description and the sentiment is denied me.'*

Popular at the time, but little read today, were the novels of **Benjamin Disraeli** (1804–1881) and **Edward Bulwer-Lytton** (1803–1873), but with the arrival on the scene of **Charles Dickens** (1812–1870) we have, of course, one of the most outstanding figures in English Literature.

Dickens was essentially a romantic and sentimentalist and believed in the novel as a way of raising awareness of social issues – unlike the other well-known writer working at the same time, **William Makepeace Thackeray** (1811–1863), whose *Barry Lyndon* (1844) and *Vanity Fair* (1846–1848) use an unsympathetic kind of realism as a deliberate antidote to the sentimentalism of Dickens and others writing in a similar vein at the time. Thackeray was much admired by **Anthony Trollope** (1815–1882), whose 1857 novel, *Barchester Towers*, is usually considered his masterpiece.

Meanwhile, up on the Yorkshire moors, three young ladies were writing novels that would become known all over the world. **Charlotte Brontë** (1816–1855) published her first novel, *Jane Eyre*, in 1847, followed by *Shirley* (1849) and *Villette* (1853), while her younger sister **Emily** (1818–1848) produced only one novel, *Wuthering Heights* (1848), but that, too, was to achieve world-wide fame. The youngest of the three sisters, **Ann** (1820–1849), wrote *Agnes Grey* (1847) and *The Tenant of Wildfell Hall* (1848), both dealing with the oppression and abuse of women.

Writing in the same period as the Brontës but in a very different vein was **Elizabeth Gaskell** (1810–1865), who vividly depicted the struggles and unjust social conditions of industrialised Britain in *Mary Barton* (1848) and *North and South* (1855), while *Cranford* (1853) is a vivid depiction of English village life of the period.

But of the great women novelists of the period, the greatest is surely **George Eliot** (Mary Ann Evans – 1819–1880). Her social observations, psychological understanding of human relationships and broad humanity have made her novels endure. *Middlemarch* (1872) is her greatest work, while *Adam Bede* (1859), *The Mill on the Floss* (1860), and *Daniel Deronda* (1876) are also magnificent.

A deeply tragic view of the human situation pervades the novels of **Thomas Hardy** (1840–1928), who was acutely aware of the difficulties of women's lives in particular. The dramatic nature of his stories and the relationships they entail have made the novels ripe for exploitation in film, notably *Far from the Madding Crowd* (novel, 1874; film 1967), *Tess of the D'Urbervilles* (novel, 1891; film 1979), and *Jude the Obscure* (novel 1896; film 1996).

The 'modern' novel is often said to begin with **Henry James** (1843–1916), born in America but settling in England. His detailed depiction of manners, psychology, relationships, and the meeting of contrasting cultures – particularly the naïve American encountering the complexities of a culturally much older Europe – along with the careful architecture of his novels, make his work well worth the effort of reading. *The Portrait of a Lady* (1881) is particularly fine, while his shorter works – including the ghost story made into an opera by Benjamin Britten, *The Turn of the Screw* (1898) – are a good place to start.

Moving into the first half of the twentieth century we have an absolute explosion of novelists to consider, but anyone wanting a basic map of the genre in this period needs to look at the following for a start …

Joseph Conrad (1857–1924) – a Polish-born seaman, writing in English, whose greatest works include *Heart of Darkness* (1899), *Lord Jim* (1900), and *Nostromo* (1904).

H. G. Wells (1866–1946) – most famous today for his science fiction novels *The Time Machine* (1895), *The Island of Doctor Moreau* (1896) and *The War of the Worlds* (1897/8). These and his other works explore wider social issues of class, Man's relationship to the physical world, and the position of women. *Kipps* (1905), *Tono-Bungay* (1909), *Ann Veronica* (1909), and *The History of Mr Polly* (1910) have remained relatively popular.

John Galsworthy (1867–1933) is largely known for *The Forsyte Saga* (published between 1906 and 1921), made into a popular television series in 1967. The effect of class on behaviour and expectations is at the heart of the work. His vision tends to be rather pessimistic, revealing how helpless most people are in the face of tradition and convention.

E. M. Forster (1879–1970) has come to many readers first through films of his novels – *Where Angels Fear to Tread* (novel 1905, film 1991), *A Room with a View* (novel 1908, film 1985), *Howards End* (novel 1910, film 1992), and *A Passage to India* (novel 1924, film 1984). Forster often presents the conflict between a sensitive, unconventional character and the world of insensitive, unimaginative convention, while the novel usually considered his greatest, *A Passage to India*, is a perceptive study of inter-racial psychology and attitudes at the time of the British Empire.

Virginia Woolf (1882–1941) knew both Forster and Henry James, but her work is very different from both. As one of the most deeply original writers of the twentieth century, it's vital to be familiar with at least some of her work. The brief *Jacob's Room* (1922) is a good place to start, but *Mrs Dalloway* (1925) and *To the Lighthouse* (1927) are recognised as the greatest. (*The Waves* [1931] is more experimental and demanding.)

James Joyce (1882–1941). His dates are the same as Virginia Woolf's, and both used forms of **stream-of-consciousness** writing, but there the similarity ends. (And Woolf didn't like Joyce's work: in terms of her contemporaries, she much preferred Proust.) Anyone who can't face *Ulysses* (1922) should try his short story collection, *Dubliners* (1914) and the semi-autobiographical novel *Portrait of the Artist as a Young Man* (1916).

D. H. Lawrence (1885–1930). Though famous for *Lady Chatterley's Lover* (1928) and the resultant **obscenity trial**, this is not considered his best novel. *Sons and Lovers* (1913) is a good place to start, while *The Rainbow* (1915) and *Women in Love* (1920) are many readers' favourites. Some of the novels can seem dated today in a world where sexual mores have radically changed. But some would put those changes down to writers like Lawrence who had the courage to tackle the subject in a new way.

Post-World War Two: The Modernist, first part of the twentieth century saw some radical experiments in the novel, but the trauma of war sent the novel back to a less adventurous 'realism' for a time. By the mid sixties, however, a greater diversity of approaches was once more emerging, proving the endless flexibility of – and many uses to which writers have put – the remarkable narrative phenomenon we call simply 'the novel'.

NOVELIST

Man or woman who spends most of their life sitting at a desk, making stuff up and hoping to get paid for it.

NOVELLA

A work of fiction shorter than an average novel, but longer than a short story. Can be very satisfying if you don't have time to wallow in long, expansive novels: you can enter more 'different worlds' in less time. Novellas might not always seem value for money because they have relatively few pages. But the costs of cover design, promotion and distribution are the same as for longer novels so it's unfair to expect a book of, say, 150 pages to be half the price of a 300-pager.

In the hands of master story-tellers, the novella can be as impressive and memorable as a full-length novel.

There are no set word-lengths to define a novella, but you can usually expect something between twenty and forty thousand words – sometimes a little more.

Famous works that are usually categorised as novellas include:

A Christmas Carol by Charles Dickens (1843)

First Love by Ivan Turgenev (1860)

The Time Machine by H. G. Wells (1895)

The Turn of the Screw by Henry James (1898)

Death in Venice by Thomas Mann (1912)

Metamorphosis by Franz Kafka (1915)

Of Mice and Men by John Steinbeck (1937)

The Snow Goose by Paul Gallico (1941)

Animal Farm by George Orwell (1945)

The Ballad of the Sad Café by Carson McCullers (1951)

The Old Man and the Sea by Ernest Hemingway (1952)

Seize the Day by Saul Bellow (1956)

Breakfast at Tiffany's by Truman Capote (1958)

A Month in the Country by J. L. Carr (1980)

O

Joyce Carol Oates – "I don't read for amusement, I read for enlightenment."

OBSCENITY TRIALS

Books have been banned or burnt for many different reasons, but not all have gone to full-scale judicial trials. Of the most famous, the earliest example is probably John Cleland's *Fanny Hill, or Memoirs of a Woman of Pleasure* (1749) – though not actually brought to trial until the early nineteenth century, when people seem to have been a little more squeamish about direct treatments of sex in the arts than their eighteenth-century forbears. We may not be surprised that such a blatantly sexy book should provoke the powers that be, but Flaubert's *Madame Bovary*? When excerpts from the novel first appeared in 1856, there was an attempt to block publication of the whole novel. The resultant law-suit was won by the author, and the entire book duly appeared in 1857. This was the same year that another great French writer, the poet Charles Baudelaire had six of the poems in his *Fleurs du mal* ('Flowers of Evil') collection banned for 'corrupting public morals' – though they appeared a few years later.

As with *Madame Bovary*, it was the publication of an excerpt from James Joyce's *Ulysses* that alerted the authorities to the pornographic nature of parts of the work. The entire book was published in 1922 by Sylvia Beach (founder of the original Shakespeare and Company bookshop in Paris). Copies were smuggled to other countries by a number of ingenious subterfuges, and it wasn't until 1934 that the US court ruling forbidding its publication there was reversed.

1928 saw the US trial of Radclyffe Hall's lesbian novel *The Well of Loneliness*, resulting in the destruction of all copies – though it's now appreciated as a literary classic … and as a useful reminder of what it was like if one's sexual identity was not mainstream in the early twentieth century. But not all obscenity trials were as disastrous as this for those finding themselves in the dock. The 1957 trial of American poet Allan Ginsburg's collection *Howl and Other Poems* helped to establish his fame.

The novel that George Orwell reckoned to be the best written in the English language to date, Henry Miller's *Tropic of Cancer* (1934), found itself in the US courts in 1961. *The God of Small Things* (1996), by Arundhati Roy, won the Booker Prize in

1997 – which didn't stop it from being hauled before the Indian courts the same year for 'corrupting public morals'. Happily, Roy won the case.

OMNISCIENT NARRATOR

Using an omniscient narrator gives the author the opportunity to present a very full picture of the world the characters inhabit and to comment upon events in the story. It goes further than simple **third person narrative** in that the omniscient ('all-knowing') narrator acts as an ever-present guide for the reader. The narrator is not necessarily to be identified with the author. The novels of George Eliot are a good example of this narrative mode – which tends to be less popular now than in the nineteenth century.

OPENINGS OF NOVELS, FAMOUS

Why is it that the openings of some novels have become really famous, and others haven't? What is it about the examples below that have caused them to stick in readers' minds? Is it simply because they are the start of great novels, or is there 'something about them' that makes them particularly memorable? How many do you recognise? (Answers below)

1 Marley was dead, to begin with.

2 It is a truth universally acknowledged, that a single man in possession of a good fortune, must be in want of a wife.

3 It was the best of times, it was the worst of times …

4 Lolita, light of my life, fire of my loins.

5 As Gregor Samsa awoke from a night of uneasy dreaming, he found himself transformed in his bed into a gigantic insect.

6 All children, except one, grow up.

7 The past is a foreign country: they do things differently there.

8 Call me Ishmael.

9 All happy families are like one another; each unhappy family is unhappy in its own way.

10 It was a bright, cold day in April and the clocks were striking thirteen.

11 Under certain circumstances there are few hours in life more agreeable than the hour dedicated to the ceremony known as afternoon tea.

12 Last night I dreamt I went to Manderley again.

13 Mother died today. Or maybe yesterday; I can't be sure.

14 Stately, plump Buck Mulligan came from the stairhead, bearing a bowl of lather on which a mirror and razor lay crossed.

15 'To be born again,' sang Gibreel Farishta tumbling from the heavens, 'first you have to die.'

ANSWERS 1. *A Christmas Carol* by Charles Dickens 2. *Pride and Prejudice* by Jane Austen 3. *A Tale of Two Cities* by Charles Dickens 4. *Lolita* by Vladimir Nabokov 5. *Metamorphosis* by Franz Kafka 6. *Peter Pan* by J. M. Barrie 7. *The Go-Between* by L. P. Hartley 8. *Moby Dick* by Herman Melville 9. *Anna Karenina* by Leo Tolstoy 10. *Nineteen Eighty-Four* by George Orwell 11. *The Portrait of a Lady* by Henry James 12. *Rebecca* by Daphne du Maurier 13. *The Outsider* by Albert Camus 14. *Ulysses* by James Joyce 15. *The Satanic Verses* by Salman Rushdie.

ORANGE PRIZE FOR LITERATURE

See **Bailey's Women's Prize for Fiction**

OULIPO

See under **Experimental Fiction** and **Fun and Games**

P

Alexander Pope – "As much company as I have kept, and as much as I love it, I love reading better, and would rather be employed in reading than in the most agreeable conversation."

PATRON SAINTS of the book world

St Francis de Sales (1567–1622) is the patron saint of writers. He is said to have been a model of good manners, sensitive to others, moderate in judgement, clear in expression, dignified and modest. (Writers, please note your role model …). He was probably chosen as the patron saint of writers because, thirty years before the actual Académie Française was established, his concern for the sciences and arts had led him to found an academy at Annency. Writers might like to note his saying, "Whoever preaches with love preaches effectively." He is celebrated on 24th January.

St Jerome (342–420) is the patron saint of librarians. He was a great biblical scholar and is famous for having made the first translation of the Bible from

Greek and Hebrew into Latin. In Rome he became leader of a group of women drawn to asceticism and a studious life, but was often disliked by people for the extreme rigour of his views and expectations and his irascible nature. Later he settled in Bethlehem and, with the financial help of the rich woman who became St Paula, opened a number of institutions including a free school where he taught Greek and Latin to local children. It's true that librarians have to be 'rigorous' (though we hope they are not 'irascible'), but we are sure St Jerome was chosen as their patron saint primarily for having made an important book available to a wider readership through his translation – just as libraries and librarians make books available to those who might not otherwise have access to them. He is celebrated on 30th September.

St John Bosco (1815–1888) is usually considered the patron saint of editors, publishers, and printers. A great admirer of St Francis de Sales (see above), he is best known for founding trade schools and is claimed as the patron saint of a number of trades. He was an effective preacher, quiet and restrained in manner. He is celebrated on 31st January.

According to some sources, the patron saint of book-sellers and printers is **Saint John of God**, though they have to share him with fire-fighters, nurses and the sick (it's true the provision of books can be 'healing', and fire-fighters might prevent books from burning ... so there might be a connection). **St John the Evangelist** is sometimes counted as the patron of papermakers. Interestingly, a number of sources also mention **St Lawrence** as a patron saint of librarians (rather than, more commonly, St Jerome). His symbol is the grid-iron, the object of his martyrdom. On a bad day, some librarians may feel this to be appropriate to their situation ...

PEN INTERNATIONAL

An international organisation, founded in 1921 by Catherine Amy Dawn Scott, campaigning for freedom of expression. The PEN charter affirms the following:

1   Literature knows no frontiers and must remain common currency among people in spite of political or international upheavals.

2   In all circumstances, and particularly in time of war, works of art, the patrimony of humanity at large, should be left untouched by national or political passion.

3   Members of PEN should at all times use what influence they have in favour of good understanding and mutual respect between nations; they pledge

themselves to do their utmost to dispel race, class and national hatreds, and to champion the ideal of one humanity living in peace in one world.

4   PEN stands for the principle of unhampered transmission of thought within each nation and between all nations, and members pledge themselves to oppose any form of suppression of freedom of expression in the country and community to which they belong, as well as throughout the world wherever this is possible. PEN declares for a free press and opposes arbitrary censorship in time of peace. It believes that the necessary advance of the world towards a more highly organised political and economic order renders a free criticism of governments, administrations and institutions imperative. And since freedom implies voluntary restraint, members pledge themselves to oppose such evils of a free press as mendacious publication, deliberate falsehood and distortion of facts for political and personal ends.

PEN's first president was novelist and playwright John Galsworthy, who wrote the first three articles of the charter. There are now PEN Centres in more than a hundred countries.

English PEN is based at the Free Word Centre in Farringdon, London. The organisation works not only to defend freedom of expression but to break down barriers between nations by actively promoting translation of worthwhile literature. It also works to remove inequalities of access to reading and creative writing by working with groups such as prisoners, refugees, and young people in disadvantaged areas.

PENGUIN: A PAPERBACK REVOLUTION

Allen Lane (1902–70), the visionary creator of Penguin Books, was inspired by the example of the German publisher Albatross Verlag who, in 1932, launched their Albatross Modern Continental Library of cheap paperbacks with colour-coded covers. It was in 1935 that Lane – with the help of a different kind of seabird – launched his imprint which, at sixpence a copy, sold three million books in its first year. By the 1950s, Penguin accounted for roughly eight per cent of British book production.

Unlike some other paperback publishers, who provided mostly **pulp fiction**, Penguin appealed to the more educated reader with high quality works by established authors of a more literary nature. And these appealed to the growing number of university graduates, particularly with the rapid expansion of university education from the 1960s onwards.

Like the German Albatross series, the original Penguin covers were simple – just typographical – and colour coded (green for crime; orange for general fiction etc). Today, Penguin Classics are easily recognisable by their distinctive black covers, although illustrations have now replaced the 'typography only' covers of the early days.

The huge success of the Penguin enterprise led to many imitators including, in France, Hachette's now famous *Livres de poche* imprint.

Many of the non-fiction texts that helped to shape a wide public knowledge of new ideas, particularly in the 1960s and 70s, appeared in Penguin's 'Pelican' imprint. The imprint's name was the result of Allen Lane overhearing, at a station bookstall, someone asking for 'one of those Pelican books', rather than a Penguin book. The idea of the Pelican's beak as being able to 'hold a great deal' also made it a suitable label. At the time of writing, Penguin have announced their intention of relaunching the series: the time is right for the spread of some big ideas.

All in all, one of the greatest success stories in publishing history, with branches of the Penguin company now established worldwide. The recent merger with the Random House Group makes it one of the most powerful publishing entities in the world.

PERSONAL LIBRARIES

The ownership of personal libraries was once the privilege of the wealthy, for whom it was often a status symbol – though among the wealthy were a number of truly learned men and women, particularly during the Renaissance period but also up to and including the eighteenth century. But the widespread rise of private home libraries – even among people living in quite humble circumstances – can be put down partly to the production of smaller-format, cloth-bound books in the nineteenth century (as opposed to the large, leather-bound tomes of previous times) which were also affordable and didn't look out of place in modest rooms. Such publications encour-aged – and were encouraged by – a growing middle-class readership. The rapid expansion of the railways and passengers' wish for books to read on long jour-neys also encouraged the production of portable volumes that would further expand their personal libraries.

Even in the twenty-first century, with the ready availability of ebooks, there are those who value their conventional personal libraries. Writer Alberto Manguel enjoys the sight of his crowded book-shelves; they form, he says, '*a sort of inventory*' of his life in which he can rediscover his past, finding in his books '*scribbles, bus tickets, scraps of paper with myste-rious names and numbers, the occasional date and place on the book's flyleaf*' taking him back to '*a certain café, a distant hotel room, a faraway summer long ago.*' Having had to abandon his personal libraries more than once in the past, he knows the pain of it – a pain as great as the late great literary critic Sir Frank Kermode must have experienced when, in the midst of moving house and having placed his packed-up, exceptional personal library in the front garden ready for the removal company, he discovered that the bin men had removed them all before the moving van arrived. More recently, Linda Grant has written movingly about the need to cull books prior to moving to smaller accommodation and, having been a little too ruthless, found herself facing not only regret but empty shelves. A cautionary tale for book-lovers …

PICARESQUE NOVEL, THE

In Spanish, *picaro* means rascal or rogue – the origin of the term 'picaresque'. Protagonists are usually some kind of anti-hero, often of a lower social class (or just down on their luck). Living by their wits, they tell their story in an episodic and usually humorous way. In fact, 'picaresque' has come to be applied loosely to any story told in an episodic manner, rather than having a tightly constructed plot.

Although the term 'picaresque' doesn't appear until the early nineteenth century, the story credited with founding the genre is the Spanish *Lazarillo de*

Tormes (author anonymous) which appeared in 1554. However, it makes use of characterisation elements already present in Roman literature, and particularly Arabic literature familiar to many Spanish readers at the time.

Novels in the picaresque manner began to appear all over Europe. In Britain, they reached their peak in the eighteenth century with works such as Daniel Defoe's *Moll Flanders* (1722) and novels by Henry Fielding (think *Joseph Andrews* [1742] and *Tom Jones* [1749]), who attributed his method to a love of Cervantes' *Don Quixote*.

Dickens, who was influenced by Fielding, wrote his first novels in the picaresque style. Other well-known nineteenth-century novels include Thackeray's *The Luck of Barry Linden* (1844), and Mark Twain's *The Adventures of Huckleberry Finn* (1884). Two notable examples from the twentieth century are Henry Miller's *Tropic of Cancer* (1934) and German writer Thomas Mann's *The Confessions of Felix Krull, Confidence Man* (1954).

PILGRIMAGES, LITERARY

Some people like them, some don't. Even if they don't change or enhance your understanding of a writer, they can be fun, especially if you find yourself holidaying nearby. Here are a few suggestions ... there are plenty more at **www.writershouses.com**. Another kind of pilgrimage is to visit the final resting place of writers. See **Writers' Graves** for some suggestions.

UK

Jane Austen's House Museum, Chawton, Alton, Hampshire. Where most of her mature work was done. Train from London Waterloo to Alton, bus to Alton Butts, 12 minute walk to Chawton Village. Or bus from Winchester Bus Station.

The Brontë Parsonage Museum, Haworth, West Yorkshire. Run by the Brontë Society. Train to Leeds, another to Keighley, bus to Haworth. One of the most famous sites of literary pilgrimage in the UK.

Lord Byron's Newstead Abbey, Ravenshead in Nottingham-shire can only be visited on Sundays and with a conducted tour.

Chaucer is represented by the Canterbury Tales Museum in Canterbury, which brings to life some of his best-loved stories. Not sophisticated, but fun.

Agatha Christie If you're near Brixham, Devon, go to her house, called 'Greenway', in Galmpton.

Charles Dickens has a museum in his only remaining London home at 48 Doughty Street, Holborn, but there's also the Charles Dickens Birthplace Museum in Portsmouth (393 Old Commercial Road), and Gad's Hill Place, Higham (near Roch-ester, Kent), open on selected days only.

Thomas Hardy His 'Wessex' is based on the modern county of Dorset. A visit to Dorchester and the surrounding countryside can help recreate the atmosphere of his novels, but his cottage is not open to the public – though you *can* visit his house 'Max

Gate', not far from Dorchester town centre, and run by the National Trust.

Henry James The National Trust runs his house in West Street, Rye, Sussex.

Samuel Johnson Visit the house where he wrote his 'Dictionary', at 17 Gough Square, London EC4 (it's up a tiny alleyway off Fleet Street, but is sign-posted).

John Keats The house where he stayed in Hampstead is beautifully preserved and hosts many literary events. Well worth a visit. (It's found in the road now called Keats Grove.)

Rudyard Kipling's lovely Jacobean house, Bateman's, in Burwash, East Sussex, is owned by the National Trust (train to Etchingham) and isn't too far from Sissinghurst Castle, the home of **Vita Sackville West** often visited by **Virginia Woolf**.

John Milton You can visit his cottage at Chalfont St Giles in Buckinghamshire.

William Morris Visit Kelmscott House in Hammersmith (West London), and the William Morris Museum in Walthamstow (East London).

Beatrix Potter If you're holidaying in the Lake District, you could visit her house, 'Hill Top', in Hawkshead, Ambleside.

William Shakespeare Obviously Stratford-upon-Avon, Warwickshire. Houses, museums, theatre, tea-rooms – soak yourself in the Bard. And go to a play at the rebuilt Globe Theatre on London's South Bank, which also houses a Shakespeare Museum and offers conducted tours of the theatre.

George Bernard Shaw's home for 44 years was the Edwardian villa at Ayot St Lawrence, Hertfordshire, known as Shaw's Corner; it's run by the National Trust. By train, it's 4½ miles from Welwyn North, 6 miles from Welwyn Garden City, and 5 miles from Harpenden.

Robert Louis Stevenson fans can find memorabilia in the Writers' Museum in Edinburgh, along with items relating to **Robert Burns** and **Sir Walter Scott**. (And if you just happen to visit Samoa, there's a lovely Stevenson Museum there, too.)

Dylan Thomas The Boathouse and Writing Shed at Laugharne, Wales – very popular with admirers of this poet.

Virginia Woolf – her Sussex home, Monk's House, Rodmell, is now run by the National Trust. 4 miles south of Lewes, 5 miles north of Newhaven. Train from London Victoria to Lewes, bus from there to Rodmell village. Woolf's London residencies can be seen from the outside and are identified by blue plaques. The original family home was at 22 Hyde Park gate. She also lived at 46 Gordon Square, 38 Brunswick Square, 29 Fitzroy Square, 52 Tavistock Square, had a flat in Mecklenburgh Square (but was bombed out in 1940), and Hogarth House in Paradise Road, Richmond-upon-Thames. Childhood holidays were spent at Talland House in St Ives, Cornwall (now turned into luxury holiday apartments) from which she saw the Godrevy lighthouse – the inspiration for her novel *To the Lighthouse*.

William Wordsworth – the tiny 'Dove Cottage' in Grasmere is a must if you're in the Lake District.

IRELAND

In Dublin, visit the Writers' Museum, as well as the **James Joyce** Tower and Museum at Sandycove, and the James Joyce Centre (and say hello to the jaunty little statue of Joyce on Grafton Street). You might like to go to an event at the **Samuel Beckett Centre** theatre, at Trinity College, in the heart of Dublin. And visit the Oscar Wilde House on Merrion Square – but don't be alarmed by the rather bizarre, highly-coloured statue of Wilde reclining on a rock in the park area around which the lovely houses of Merrion Square are built.

FRANCE

If you're in Paris, go to the **Victor Hugo** museum in the Place des Vosges, **Balzac**'s house in Passy (47 rue Raynouard – métro Passy or Avenue du Président Kennedy) and the **Musée de la Vie Romantique**, at the foot of the Montmartre hill, which has a number of literary associations. (There's also a Balzac museum at the Château de Saché in Touraine.) About halfway between Paris and Le Mans, south west of Paris and not too far from Chartres, you can visit the House of Aunt Léonie which features in the important opening sections of M**arcel Proust**'s *In Search of Lost Time*. It's in the village of Illiers – now rechristened, in honour of Proust's novel and with an eye to tourism, Illiers-Combray. It's at 4, rue du Docteur Proust. If you're near Périgord, in the Dordogne, go to the famous tower where **Montaigne** (father of the **essay**) worked – it's open to visitors – part of the Château de Montaigne. It's possible – but quite difficult – to get there by public transport. And there's **Emile Zola**'s house at 26 rue Pasteur, in Médan (the north-western suburbs of Paris), and **Voltaire**'s Château de Cirey, in Cirey-sur-Blaise (in the Haute-Marne region of north-eastern France).

OTHER EUROPEAN LOCATIONS

If in Madrid, go to the **Cervantes** birthplace museum; in Amsterdam, visit the **Anne Frank** House; in Frankfurt and Weimar, there are **Goethe** museums; the **Ibsen** Museum is in Oslo, Norway; in Prague, visit the **Kafka** birthplace and museum; in Rome, the **Keats-Shelley** house can be found on the Piazza di Spagna.

RUSSIA

The beautiful old house of **Leo Tolstoy**, Yasnaya Polyana, is a must (it's 12km south-west of Tula and about 200 km from Moscow). Moscow is also where you'll find the **Chekhov** Museum and, at Peredelkino, in the Moscow region, the **Boris Pasternak** Museum. And if you're in St Petersburg, there's the **Pushkin** Apartment Museum (12 River Moika), the **Dostoyevsky** Literary Memorial Museum on Kuznechay Lane, as well as museums dedicated to more recent writers, the poets **Anna Akhmatova** and **Joseph Brodsky**.

USA

In New York, visit Poe Cottage, **Edgar Allan Poe**'s home in the Bronx (Kingsbridge Road) – and you can also visit his 'basement' in Philadelphia. There's a museum dedicated to **Eudora Welty** in Jackson, Mississippi, and in the same state, 'Rowan Oak', in Oxford, dedicated to **William Faulkner**. Massachusetts has the house of **Herman Melville** ('Arrowhead') in Pittsfield, and 'The Mount', home of **Edith Wharton** (the first woman novelist to win a **Pulitzer Prize**) in Lenox. **Mark Twain**'s boyhood home on Main Street, Hannibal Missouri (north east of St Louis) is a museum, as is **Flannery O'Connor**'s 'Andalusia Farm' in Milledgeville, Georgia. If you like **Emily Dickinson**'s poetry, visit 280 Main Street, Amherst, Massachusetts. The **Ernest Hemingway** home and museum is in Whitehead Street, Key West, Florida. And fans of **F. Scott Fitzgerald** and **Zelda Fitzgerald** will find their museum on

Felder Avenue in Montgomery, Alabama. There are several places to visit to pay tribute to the author of *Little Women* (and the sequels), **Louisa May Alcott**: all are in Massachusetts: 'Fruitlands Farmhouse', Prospect Hill, Harvard; 'The Wayside', Lexington Road, Concord; 'Orchard House', also in Lexington Road; but the Alcott family house in Boston (Pinchney Street) can only be viewed from the outside as it's not open to the public.

PLAGIARISM

The act of 'stealing' material from another author's work and passing it off as one's own. Although plagiarism isn't actually a criminal offence, it is likely to infringe copyright laws, and is certainly frowned upon by the literary community as being deeply unethical. There have been some famous cases of plagiarism, even by the great French writer Stendhal. Helen Keller appears to have committed accidental plagiarism and decided the best way to avoid it was to write her autobiography which, by its very nature, would be 'original'. Alex Haley was accused of plagiarism in connection with his famous novel *Roots*, while the most recent controversy was that surrounding Dan Brown's *The Da Vinci Code*.

POET

In the popular imagination, poets tend to be poor, unkempt, intense, alcoholic (Dylan Thomas) or on drugs (Coleridge wrote 'Kubla Khan' under the influence of) and considerably more given to suicide than the rest of the population. But the fact is that many great poets held down a day job. Geoffrey Chaucer (1340–1400), known as the father of English poetry, was not only a soldier, a spy, and an international diplomat, he was also controller of customs for the Port of London and Clerk of the King's Works. John Donne was Dean of St Paul's; Keats was a qualified surgeon (though he didn't actually practice); Matthew Arnold was a schools' inspector; William Carlos Williams was a family doctor; T. S. Eliot worked in a bank (Lloyds) then at a publishers (Faber and Faber); Stevie Smith was a secretary; Louis MacNeice worked for the BBC; Wallace Stevens was an insurance company executive, and Philip Larkin a librarian. Russian poet Yevgeny Yevtushenko was a keen footballer in his youth. Hardly the clichéd image of the neurasthenic poet.

POET LAUREATE

An ancient institution that goes back to the middle ages, the poet laureate is the official poetic voice of the nation. But being chosen as Britain's 'poet laureate' (from the laurel wreath that was traditionally awarded to competition victors in Classical times) is both an honour and a mixed blessing. It's an honour because it puts you in a long line of eminent poets and your place in literary history is probably assured; a mixed blessing because of what the post unofficially entails. Although there is no absolute requirement to do so, the holder of the post is expected to write verses for significant national occasions and, these days, to be seen to promote poetry in various ways (Andrew Motion did some excellent work in schools). A small annual payment is received (currently about £6,000) and although the post was once held 'for life', it is now for a term of ten years.

A number of poets have turned down the offer (including Philip Larkin), but only one has been 'relieved of his duties' – John Dryden was thrown out in 1688 for refusing to swear an oath of allegiance to the new king, William III. The last ten laureates and the years in which they were appointed are as follows: Carol Ann Duffy (2009), Andrew Motion (1999), Ted Hughes (1984), John Betjeman (1972), Cecil Day-Lewis (1968), John Masefield (1930), Robert Bridges (1913), Alfred Austin (1896), Alfred Lord Tennyson (1850), William Wordsworth (1843).

POETRY

Most of us need to read more of it.

If all the people who write poetry – of whatever kind – were to buy and read books of other people's poetry, there would be two clear advantages:

1   Their own poetry would almost certainly improve

2   Publishers of contemporary poetry would not be so poverty-stricken and have to rely on grants and the kindness of strangers.

POETRY LIBRARY, THE

Located in the Festival Hall (Level 5), part of London's South Bank Centre, the Poetry Library is a wonderful resource available to the public. It was founded in 1953 by the Arts Council and has more than 200,000 items dating from 1912 to the present day and is *the* major library for modern and contemporary poetry.

The library aims to stock all poetry published in the UK, along with a selection of poetry from other countries, some in parallel text, some just in English translation. It also holds a vast store of the **little magazines** which have been, and continue to be, important for emerging poets in particular. Material is available in many formats, including electronic, of course, and there is also a thriving children's section. Well worth a visit.

PRINT ON DEMAND (POD)

A useful recent innovation on the publishing scene, particularly for smaller publishers or individuals.

The sophistication of modern print technology means that large print-runs that might not sell – and the resultant waste of money and resources – can be avoided. (Some large bookshops even have their own POD machines.)

PRIX GONCOURT

The most prestigious of French literary prizes, it's been awarded every year since 1903. The Goncourt brothers were famous in the literary world of the nineteenth century and Edmond de Goncourt (author and publisher – his diaries are a fascinating record of the period and readily available) left his estate for the founding of the *Académie Goncourt* and the sponsoring of the prize for 'the best and most imaginative prose work of the year'.

As well as the main prize, there are others for a first novel, a short story, poetry and biography. The prize money is negligible, but winning the Goncourt assures the author of huge book sales which more than makes up for it. Winners likely to be familiar to English readers include Marcel Proust (1871–1922 – won 1919); Elsa Triolet (1896–1970 – won 1944); Simone de Beauvoir (1908–1986 – won 1954); Henri Troyat (1911–2007 – won 1938); and Marguerite Duras (1914–1996 – won 1984).

PRIZES (LITERARY)

It's not just the prize money that authors benefit from when they win a literary prize: it always significantly increases sales. With the highest profile prizes, even being on the shortlist can bring huge benefits. Of the many UK prizes, the following are generally considered the most prestigious (in alphabetical – not prestige – order):

The Bailey's Prize for Fiction by Women – Formerly the Orange Prize.

The Betty Trask Award – to writers under 35, for a traditional or romantic novel.

British Book Awards – known as the **Nibbies**.

The Costa Book Awards (the 'Costas') – formerly the Whitbread Awards.

The Folio Prize – first awarded 2014, it was established to be a more seriously literary award than the Booker, which some felt had come to prioritise readability over literary excellence.

The Hawthornden Prize – is for writers under 41 and is awarded for a broad range of genres. The prize money is modest, but the prestige makes up for it!

The Orwell Prize – (after George Orwell) is for political writing.

The Samuel Johnson Prize – is for non-fiction.

The Somerset Maugham Award – is for writers under 35, the prize money for travel.

The most prestigious poetry awards are the **Forward Prize** and the **T. S. Eliot Prize**. Poets can also be awarded a **Hawthornden Prize**.

PROJECT GUTENBERG

Named after **Johannes Gutenberg**, the person mainly responsible for instigating moveable type printing in the fifteenth century, 'Project Gutenberg' was founded in 1971 by American Michael S. Hart (d.2011) with the aim of making as many copy-right-free texts as possible available via the Internet. Right from its early, experimental stages it was run by volunteers, and there are now more than 42,000 texts just sitting there, waiting for us … They can be accessed via **www.gutenberg.org**. A truly wonderful resource.

PUBLISHERS

… are your servants, dear reader – though one can be forgiven for thinking that some of them are the servants of their shareholders and operate increasingly for the fast buck. It is said that, in some publishing houses, the Marketing Department is now in charge of which books are accepted for publication and that the role of the traditional Commissioning Editor has become so minimal that they frequently double as office cleaner. (Not that we're cynical …)

Because of the pressure to achieve large profit margins, publishers can no longer nurture the promising new writer, nor maintain what was previously known as their 'mid list' – writers whose work just trotted along steadily but modestly in terms of sales and prestige … somewhere between Mills and Boon and a Booker nominee, let's say.

And they really don't want books that need editing. They want them up and running and ready to go. Much of the sifting work that once upon a time fell upon the editorial department is now done by **literary agents**.

PUBLISHING INDUSTRY

It's actually thriving, despite recurring apocalyptic prognostications about the death of the novel, the death of the *book*, the decline of reading *et cetera*, *et cetera*. Yes, it has changed, is changing, and will go on changing – like any healthy organism. Flexibility has to be the watch-word in any viable industry. And to judge by the number of talented and ambitious young people who want to 'get into publishing' – despite the insecurity and sometimes abysmal salaries – it must have *something* going for it!

PULITZER PRIZE

The most famous American literary prize (though

it's also awarded for journalism and music). It was founded as a result of the will of Hungarian-born American publisher Joseph Pulitzer and the prizes have been awarded annually since 1917 (announced in April). Winners whose work will be familiar to world-wide audiences include poets Robert Frost and Robert Lowell, playwrights Eugene O'Neill, Edward Albee, Thornton Wilder and Tennessee Williams, and novelists William Faulkner, Norman Mailer and John Updike.

PULP FICTION

A term for cheap, low quality fiction. It comes from the cheap wood pulp paper on which such fiction is printed. In the first half of the twentieth century, there were many 'pulp' magazines, particularly in the USA. The term is probably best known today through the title of Quentin Tarantino's film *Pulp Fiction*.

Q

Raymond Queneau – "One can easily classify all works of fiction as descendants of either the *Iliad* or the *Odyssey*."

QUALITY FICTION

(see **Literary Fiction**.)

'QUICK READS'

These are short, easy-to-read books by well-known authors, written specifically for those adults (one in six of the population) who find reading difficult (or boring) for various reasons.

Since 2006, the 'Quick Reads' project has distributed more than 4.5 million books, has registered more than 3 million library loans and, through outreach work, has created hundreds of thousands of new readers. In so doing it has been changing people's lives through the benefits of reading and giving them the confidence to 'take up a book'. They are readily available from bookshops, libraries and can be ordered on line.

QUIET CARRIAGE

A human right. Use it. Defend it.

QUIXOTE, DON

See **Don Quixote Syndrome**

QUOTING

One of the benefits of an 'old-fashioned' education was being obliged to learn lots of poems – and even passages of prose – by heart. This gave a large store of treasures to draw on throughout life. The joyful sight of daffodils in spring is enhanced by having the observations and emotions of Wordsworth's '*I wandered lonely as a cloud*' readily to hand. And as soon as the lilac comes out, lines from T. S. Eliot's *The Waste Land* – '*Now that lilacs are in bloom/She has a bowl of lilacs in her room* … ' – can't help but run through one's head. Feeling the sad burden of one's mortality while gazing at the sea, one might be a little comforted by the universality of that feeling caught in the opening of Shakespeare's sonnet, '*Like as the waves make towards the pebbled shore / So do our minutes hasten to their end.*'

But quoting should probably be confined mainly to one's own head – or to the presence of a close friend who may share and understand one's frame of literary reference. Scattering quotations from literature through one's general conversation is not a good idea – it sounds like showing off. But the occasional, well-placed quote is acceptable, and can be useful.

R

John Ruskin – "Life being very short, and the quiet hours of it few, we ought to waste none of them in reading valueless books."

READING DIARIES

Keeping a reading diary can be a useful and enjoyable way of recording our reactions to books – and nice to look back on. There are also a number of published reading diaries worth looking at (even if you don't take them as a model for your own) including:

A Reading Diary: A Year of Favourite Books (2004). Alberto Manguel re-reads one of his favourite books each month – an eclectic mix that includes *The Wind in the Willows*, Margaret Atwood's *Surfacing*, a Conan Doyle story, and books by Goethe, Chateaubriand, Kipling and H. G. Wells – and *Don Quixote*, of course.

Howards End is on the Landing: A Year of Reading from Home (2009). Novelist and short story writer Susan Hill records a wide range of her reading and re-reading through twelve months, and turns it into a passionate advocacy for reading.

An Everywhere: A Little Book About Reading (Heather Reyes, 2014). This records a three-month period of intense reading as 'bibliotherapy' in a difficult situation, also considering wider issues of reading and writing that emerge from the books encountered.

READER GROUPS/BOOK GROUPS

A phenomenon that has spread like wild-fire in recent years, much to the joy of publishers and librarians. Reader groups come in many flavours, many shapes, many sizes, and it's important to choose the right one for you if you're going to get the most out of it. Obviously, if you're a rather sensitive soul who can't stand the smell of beer, there's no point joining a rumbustious group that meets in a pub to talk about the latest crime thrillers.

It's true that most reader group members are women – but then women are, generally, bigger readers than men. But the gentlemen are beginning to notice the pleasure and enrichment to be had from book groups and are gradually getting in on the act. Before joining a group, it's a good idea to find out what books they have been reading recently, to make sure they are fairly compatible with your own taste – though sometimes, of course, it's good to be taken in new directions. Maybe ask if you can sit in on a meeting of the group before 'committing', to make sure the level of discussion – and the personalities of the members – are going to be right for you.

> **Talking Point**   What are the particular pleasures of belonging to a reader group? Are there any down sides or difficulties in belonging to such a group?

READING IN THE BATH

If you must – but please not library books or books borrowed from unsuspecting friends because the inevitable will, one day, certainly happen …

READING ON THE LOO

If faking constipation is the only way you can get a quiet moment to yourself to read, then so be it …

And here's Franz Kafka on the subject: '*You are not allowed to think of the Torah in the toilet, and for this reason you may read worldly books there. A very pious man in Prague, a certain K., knew a great deal of the worldly sciences; he had studied them all in the toilet.*'

READING ON TRAINS

Yes, some people still do it – or try to. Apart from newspapers, old-fashioned books are still favourite, though a growing number of e-readers are in evidence.

But you will often find yourself in competition with mobile phone users brazenly revealing the most intimate details of their personal lives (or just what they had for lunch) or doing low-level business deals or simply taking the opportunity to 'touch base' with friends as there is clearly nothing else to do on a train and of course the lady opposite doesn't mind: she's only reading, after all!

Possible solution: if you are able to listen to music at the same time as reading – some people can – then put your i-pod in your ears and try to create some 'personal space'. Or, for long journeys, make sure you book a seat in the 'quiet carriage' (which tends to be a relative term …).

READING TO CHILDREN

… is as important as keeping them clean and fed.

As soon as their eyes can focus, sit the baby on your lap and, with the help of the many wonderful books produced for the purpose, initiate them into the world of books.

But even when they start to be able to read for themselves, keep reading to them as well: children's ability to enter into the worlds of stories is usually more developed than their actual reading abilities and they can lose the pleasure of books if frustrated by the gap between what they can understand and enjoy and what they are actually able to read for themselves. Besides, it's fun, reading to kids!

REALISM

In literature, 'Realism' is the term applied to much fiction that emerged notably in France in the early to mid-nineteenth century with writers such as Honoré de Balzac (1799–1850) and Gustave Flaubert (1821–1880). Such writing emphasises the details of everyday, usually contemporary life in a non-romanticised manner. In terms of British writing, George Eliot (1819–1880) is its finest nineteenth-century representative and *Middlemarch* (1874) her greatest novel.

RECOMMENDING BOOKS TO FRIENDS

A word of warning from playwright Henry Miller: '*Have you noticed, after many heartaches and disillusionments, that in recommending a book to a friend the less said the better? The moment you praise a book too highly you awaken resistance in your listener.*'

REJECTION LETTERS

It's a lot harder to get a book published than most people realise. All authors are familiar with the phenomenon of 'the rejection letter' – that nasty little envelope (or email) that, after a long period of waiting (usually) comes back from the publisher. Many struggling authors comfort themselves with stories of famous writers being rejected. Here are just a few famous examples from rejection letters received by subsequently acclaimed authors:

J. G. Ballard – (re. *Crash*) '*The author of this book is beyond psychiatric help.*'

Emily Dickinson – '*[Your poems] are quite as remarkable for their defects as for beauties and are generally devoid of true poetical qualities.*'

F. Scott Fitzgerald – '*You'd have a decent book if you'd get rid of that Gatsby character.*'

William Golding – (re. *Lord of the Flies*) '*An absurd and uninteresting fantasy which was rubbish and dull.*'

Ernest Hemingway – (re. *Torrents of Spring*) '*It would be extremely rotten taste, to say nothing of being horribly cruel, should we want to publish it.*'

Rudyard Kipling – '*I'm sorry, Mr Kipling, but you just don't know how to use the English language.*'

D. H. Lawrence – (re. *Lady Chatterley's Lover*) '*For your own sake, do not publish this book.*'

Vladimir Nabokov – (re. *Lolita*) '*I recommend that it be buried under a stone for a thousand years.*'

Sylvia Plath – '*There certainly isn't enough genuine talent for us to take notice.*'

George Orwell had trouble finding a publisher for *Animal Farm* and one of the reasons given was 'it's impossible to sell animal stories in the USA'. **John le Carré**, submitting *The Spy Who Came in from the Cold* was told he hadn't got any future in writing. **Ursula Le Guin**'s famous *The Left Hand of Darkness* was dismissed as 'unreadable', **C. S. Lewis** received 800 rejections before selling his first piece of writing, and Pat Barker took ten years to find a publisher for *Union Street*. When Nobel Prize winner **Alice Munro** submitted her wonderful short story collection *Dance of the Happy Shades*, the response was that there was 'nothing particularly new and exciting' about the stories, and moreover, the author was 'not that young'!!!

REPS

Or, more properly, 'Book Sales Representatives', are something of a vanishing breed these days with so much information and book promotion happening via the Internet. But they still have a valuable role in maintaining personal contact between buyers/book-shop managers and the publisher. The reps' personal knowledge of and (one hopes) enthusiasm for the books they are representing can make a real difference to the process of 'selling in' to bookshops. Spending their working lives on the road, often covering very large territories, they are still among the heroes of the book world.

RE-READING

Re-reading a favourite book at different times of life can reveal a lot about the changes experience has effected in us. But re-reading doesn't come without risks: a book we were passionate about in youth may not stand the test of time – we might see through its narrative devices or find the character we *so* identified with to be callow and shallow. But re-reading truly great novels can be hugely enriching as we are in a position, after having lived a bit, to truly appreciate the detailed perceptions and insights of the author. Writer and historian of reading Alberto Manguel spent a whole year re-reading some of this favourite books and recording his reactions, and wrote about the experience in *A Reading Diary: A Year of Favourite Books* (2005).

> **ADVICE** Usually better to re-read one really great book than to try **keeping up with the literary Joneses** by reading piles of less-than-great stuff published week after week: no harm waiting to see if they will stand the test of time.

REVIEWS/REVIEWERS

Reviews of books in newspapers and magazines have been the traditional way for the reading public to learn about the latest books. They come in all flavours, from the bitterly destructive to the cloyingly laudatory – though most are somewhere in the middle, pointing out weaknesses, but giving due praise to strengths. The best reviews are informative (without, in the case of novels, giving too much away) with a sense of the reviewer's genuine engagement with the book – and they should help you decide if this book is for you.

Most reviewers, these days, prefer to err on the side of generosity, rather than being fiercely critical – an attitude summed up by prolific American writer Joyce Carol Oates: '*If a book I've committed myself to review turns out to be 'disappointing', I make an effort to present it objectively to the reader, including a good number of excerpts from the text, so that the reader might form his or her own opinion independent of my own.*'

Unfortunately, the space given to reviewing books in the daily press – even in the broadsheets – is shrinking as films, DVDs, CDs etc take over the space. But for those who enjoy fuller, more detailed reviews there is the excellent *London Review of Books*, and the *New York Review of Books*.

And the internet has provided a whole new dimension to book reviewing as anyone can post a book review on the Amazon site, for example, or start a **book blog** for the purposes of reviewing. This is a very 'democratic' approach to reviewing, even if the quality of the reviews varies. Good reviewing is a skilled business – though sometimes the enthusiasm of the amateur can be refreshing and helpful.

Writing one's own review of a book just finished can be a useful way of considering and clarifying one's responses, even if you don't publish it online or even show it to anyone else.

ROMAN À CLEF

The French term used to denote a 'novel with a key', in which real events and people are disguised as fiction. (The 'key' is, of course, knowing which character stands for which actual person.) Although the genre has tentative beginnings at least as far back as the seventeenth century, the first example likely to be familiar to English readers is Lady Caroline Lamb's *Glenarvon* (1816), a portrayal of her affair with (a thinly disguised) Lord Byron. In *The Green Carnation* (1894), Robert Hitchens fictionalises the relationship between Oscar Wilde and Lord Alfred Douglas. H. G. Wells' affair with Amber Reeves is the subject of his *Ann Veronica* (1909), while W. Somerset Maugham creates, in *The Moon and Sixpence* (1919), a story that closely parallels the life of artist Paul Gauguin (especially the part when he leaves his wife and family and goes off to the South Seas to paint). Other famous twentieth-century examples include Ernest Hemingway's *The Sun Also Rises* (1926), a fictionalised portrait of his very real literary life in Paris, Virginia Woolf's *Orlando*

(1928) – a 'tribute' to Vita Sackville-West – George Orwell's *Animal Farm* (1954) – a rather unusual use of the genre in that it uses animals to represent specific historical figures in recent Russian history – and, in the same year, Simone de Beauvoir's *The Mandarins*. Sylvia Plath's portrayal of her own breakdown and suicide attempt is vividly novelised in *The Bell Jar* (1963). *Primary Colours* (1996), a disguised account of Bill Clinton's presidential campaign, was originally published anonymously, though later revealed to be by Joe Klein. John Banville's *The Untouchable* (1997) is a fictionalised biography of spy Anthony Blunt.

The origins of the genre lay with a wish to avoid hurt, scandal, or legal proceedings, but can also be a source of creative freedom to deal with 'the problematic real' in an informative, thought-provoking and entertaining way.

ROMANCE

Basically, he, she, and it – from Mills and Boon to Jane Austen. Like all genres, it has its sub-categories, such as Historical Romance, Science Fiction Romance, Fantasy Romance, Lesbian Romance. And **chick-lit** often has a 'romance' element. There's usually a happy ending: nobody takes arsenic …

ROMAN-FLEUVE

Meaning 'river novel', this is the French equivalent of the less metaphoric English term 'novel sequence' – basically, a series of novels that shares characters, settings, and themes, though each novel in the sequence has its own title and forms a coherent narrative in itself. Two of the most famous French examples from the nineteenth century are Honoré de Balzac's *La Comédie humaine* and Émile Zola's Rougon-Macquart cycle, while the early twentieth century gave us Marcel Proust's magnificent *In Search of Lost Time*, and, later, Jean-Paul Sartre's *Roads to Freedom*. Well-known English examples include Anthony Trollope's Palliser novels, Anthony Powell's *A Dance to the Music of Time*, Lawrence Durrell's *Alexandria Quartet* and Paul Scott's *Raj Quartet*. Two other notable examples are John Updike's Rabbit Angstrom books, and *The Cairo Trilogy* by Egyptian Naquib Mahfouz. And there are many, many more ...

S

Logan Pearsall Smith – "People say that life is the thing, but I prefer reading."

SCANDINAVIAN NOIR

Sometimes referred to as 'Nordic Noir'. A crime fiction genre written by Scandinavian writers with a Scandinavian setting in which the mood is particularly dark and the moral universe in which the stories take place a complex one. Typically using a very stripped-down style, the genre has seen phenomenal success in recent years. Swedish author Stieg Larsson's posthumously published trilogy (he died of a heart attack after climbing stairs to his office when the lift was out of order) – *The Girl With The Dragon Tattoo*, *The Girl Who Played With Fire* and *The Girl Who Kicked The Hornet's Nest* – has been a huge success worldwide. Along with Norwegian Jo Nesbö and Danish Peter Höeg, Larsson has been responsible for establishing the genre's popularity. The filming for television of Swedish writer Henning Mankell's Wallander novels (with Kenneth Branagh as police inspector Kurt Wallander) has helped to popularise the genre even further.

SCIENCE FICTION

The genre of Science Fiction – or SciFi (or just SF) – refers to stories with futuristic settings, sometimes involving space or time travel (though not always) or extraterrestrial life. But such settings and events are often used to explore serious issues of the terrestrial world. There are many subgenres within the category: a few examples – Hard SF, which pays close attention to accurate scientific detail; Soft (or 'Social') SF with a focus on social and/or psychological issues, including dystopian futuristic narratives (such as Aldous Huxley's *Brave New World* [1932], George Orwell's *Nineteen Eight-Four* [1949], and Margaret Atwood's *The Handmaid's Tale* [1985]); and Space Opera (mainly set on distant planets or in outer space, with large-scale conflicts of an 'heroic' nature). Other more recent subgenres include Feminist Science Fiction, Cyberpunk, Biopunk and Steampunk.

Devotees of Science Fiction will often subscribe to fan publications and attend SciFi conventions. In the past, the genre has been dominated by male writers – and readers – but this has been changing in recent decades.

Some of the most famous Science Fiction writers of the past (in addition to those mentioned above) and examples of their work are as follows:

Jules Verne (1828–1905) *Journey to the Centre of the Earth* (1864), *Twenty Thousand Leagues Under the Sea* (1870).

H. G. Wells (1866–1946) *The Time Machine* (1895), *War of the Worlds* (1898).

John Wyndham (1903–1969) *The Day of the Triffids* (1951), *The Kraken Wakes* (1953), *The Chrysalids* (1955), *The Midwich Cuckoos* (1957).

Arthur C. Clarke (1917–2008) Too many to name, but probably best known for *2001: A Space Odyssey* – partly as a result of Stanley Kubrick's film. (The book was written alongside the film and not published until after it.)

Frank Herbert (1920–1986) *Dune* (1965).

Isaac Asimov (1920–1992) A huge number!

Ray Bradbury (1920–2012) *Farenheit 451* (1953).

Brian Aldiss (b.1925) Very many, including the *Helliconia Trilogy* (1982, 1983, 1985).

Ursula K. Le Guin (b.1929) *The Left Hand of Darkness* (1969), *The Dispossessed* (1974).

J. G. Ballard (1930–2009) *The Drowned World* (1962), *The Burning World* (1964).

William Gibson (b.1948) *Neuromancer* (1984).

Douglas Adams (1952—2001) Comic science fiction series: *The Hitch-Hiker's Guide to the Galaxy* (1979), *The Restaurant at the End of the Universe* (1980), *Life, the Universe and Everything* (1982), *So Long and Thanks for All the Fish* (1984), *Mostly Harmless* (1992).

Iain M. Banks (1954–2013) A number written over 25 years centring on 'the Culture', the earliest being *Consider Phlebas* (1987), the last being *The Hydrogen Sonata* (2012).

SECOND-HAND BOOKS

Even people who wouldn't dream of wearing second-hand clothes will happily buy and read second-hand books – which range from those dubious-looking, battered little paperbacks (5 for £1) in cardboard boxes on a pavement table in front of the shop to the most expensive collectors' items from specialist dealers in **antiquarian books**. The former may demonstrate their anonymous reading history with coffee stains, grease marks, and occasional crumbs caught between pages; the latter will possibly have their history of ownership recorded in bookplates or inscriptions, and stains will be mainly **foxing** or similar, unavoidable depredations of time.

Between the two extremes are the vast majority of second-hand books sold, their previous owners often indicated by touching dedications from family or friends on birthdays, Christmases, as 'thank yous' or in memory of a happy time spent together – and sometimes given as a school or college prize. These can be real tear-jerkers. All that love and thoughtfulness ending up in a second-hand bookshop, looking at you like those doe-eyed puppies in old-fashioned pet shops, just asking to be bought and loved again …

But sometimes you have to harden your heart. Depending on how they have been stored, second-hand books can sometimes exude a distinct odour. Have too many on your shelves and your home will begin to smell like that musty little second-hand bookshop you remember haunting in your youth during a particularly wet holiday in a little seaside town …

SECONDHAND BOOK SHOPS

The term can, technically, cover everything from the expensive, highly specialist antiquarian book-seller to your local Oxfam bookshop. But for many book-lovers – especially those of a certain age – the words 'secondhand bookshop' conjures up a certain smell, a certain fusty crowdedness and cramped-ness, and the magic of discovering the very same edition of that book you studied in school (you just *have* to rescue it), or a replacement for that novel you loaned to you can't remember who but they never returned it and its absence has spoiled your otherwise complete set of the author's work. So, yes, you have to have it.

But of course there are many secondhand book-shops that sell mainly more recent books. Main-stream bookshops don't always stock an author's **backlist** – unless they are among the literary giants – and the secondhand shop can be a good place to pick these up, if you don't want to use Amazon.

And browsing in a good secondhand bookshop can also provide a lesson in the history of publishing …

> **WARNING** If you suffer from asthma, the old-fashioned secondhand bookshop, with its mustiness and dustiness, may need to be avoided.

SELF-PUBLISHED NOVELS

Virginia Woolf did it (and got her sister to design the covers); James Joyce did it (with a bit of help from his friend Sylvia Beach); even Marcel Proust, Leo Tolstoy, Ernest Hemingway and Gertrude Stein did it – and lots of others, too, at various points in their careers. And today, with the help of the web and other easy-to-use technology, the self-published novel is one of the most significant new publishing phenomena.

Standard book production has fallen increasingly into the hands of a few vast publishing conglomerates whose high overheads and share-holder demands make it ever more difficult for them to gamble on new, unknown writers. As a result, some of the most interesting new work is being brought out by small (not to say tiny) publishers – or even by the writers themselves. The case of *Fifty Shades of Grey* will, of course, go down in publishing history.

But would-be writers beware: for every self-publishing success, hundreds – and possibly thousands – of self-published books languish unread, unloved, and unprofitable. So, while it's easier to 'make' a book these days, you still have to flog it. Marketing and promotion take time and energy, but are absolutely vital.

SERIALISATION

Ever wondered why some of those nineteenth-century novels are *so* long? Many of them were first published as instalments (weekly or monthly) in newspapers or magazines, the author being paid for each episode. Alexander Dumas managed to hang out *The Three Musketeers* for 139 instalments, while in Britain, the roaring success of Dickens' *The Pickwick Papers* (1836) did much to establish serialisation as a publishing mode, even for 'good' literature – which could thus reach a wider audience than if it only appeared in full book form. Flaubert's *Madame Bovary*, Tolstoy's *Anna Karenina*, Dostoyevsky's *The Brothers Karamazov*, and Harriet Beecher Stowe's *Uncle Tom's Cabin* all appeared first in serialised form. More recently, an early version of Tom Wolfe's novel *The Bonfire of the Vanities* (1987) was first published in 27 episodes.

Some magazines still carry 'serials', but the format is rarely used today for work of a more literary nature.

SHORT STORY, THE

Henry James observed that the form of the short story is placed *'at that exquisite point where poetry ends and reality begins'*. Because the form demands compression, we usually have to read more 'actively', filling the gaps in information from our own imaginations and experience of life which the more expansive form of the novel allows the writer to provide for us. We have to be fully alert to all the subtle clues of the writer's well-honed language – similar to when we read poetry – while engaging with a narrative situation.

The short story is often felt to play second fiddle to the novel (and is thought, by some, to have its origin in the folk tale), though there have been attempts to reverse this in recent years, and the awarding of the Nobel Prize for Literature to the Canadian short-story writer, Alice Munro, in 2013 may well lead to a renaissance of the genre.

If you want to read the short story at its best, look at the great classic masters of the genre, including Alexander Pushkin, Edgar Alan Poe, Nikolai Gogol, Ivan Turgenev, Guy de Maupassant, Anton Chekhov, Henry James, James Joyce, Katherine Mansfield, Franz Kafka, D. H. Lawrence, Ernest Hemingway, Raymond Carver, J. D. Salinger, Jorge Luis Borges,

Vladimir Nabokov, Flannery O'Connor, Italo Calvino and, of course, Alice Munro.

It's possible to see two main traditions in the form – the more realistic or Chekhovian story, and the story that takes us into the more fantastic reaches of the imagination, as in the Borgesian mode. One of the great advantages of the short story form is that it can transport us for a brief, intense time into an experience or way of thinking that might be difficult to sustain for the length of a novel.

If you haven't previously been 'into' short stories but would like to taste a few of the best, frequent recommendations include Gogol's 'The Overcoat', Chekhov's 'The Lady with the Dog' (sometimes translated as 'Lady with Lap-dog'); Maupassant's 'Madame Tellier's Establishment' (there's a delightful French film based on it), Katherine Mansfield's 'The Garden Party', James Joyce's 'The Dead' (from his *Dubliners* collection), and J. D. Salinger's 'For Esme, with Love and Squalor' and 'A Perfect Day for a Banana Fish'. Enjoy!

> **TALKING POINT**   Can a really good short story make as big an impact as a novel?

SHOUT LINE

A short, punchy statement on the cover of a book designed to increase the likelihood of your wanting to buy it. e.g. '*This book will change your life.*' These will sometimes be quoted remarks from a well-known personality or reviewer, sometimes a result of the publisher's marketing department coming up with a memorable and impressive statement they know will grab the attention of potential readers. Sometimes they are true.

SILENCE

Please can we have quiet rooms in libraries – like we have **quiet carriages** on trains.

SOUTHERN GOTHIC

A sub-genre of Gothic fiction set in the southern states of the USA. The stories usually involve eccentric characters, grotesque or macabre situations, and settings characterised by ugliness or decay. The sinister events often spring from situations of alienation and poverty. Using the Gothic genre to explore the social and political issues of the area, Southern Gothic can be seen to go beyond the 'shudder-inducing' function of much mainstream Gothic fiction.

Key authors associated with the Southern Gothic include Carson McCullers, William Faulkner, Flannery O'Connor, and Tennessee Williams. The best writers in the genre give their work implications beyond the issues of the Southern States in which the stories are set.

For a taste of Southern Gothic, try Carson McCullers' *The Heart is a Lonely Hunter* or *The Ballad of the Sad Café*, William Faulkner's *The Sound and the Fury* or Tennessee Williams' play *A Streetcar Named Desire*.

SPECULATIVE FICTION

A general term for genres that move beyond the everyday world of the real – such as various forms of **fantasy writing**, **science fiction**, and **horror**.

SPLIT PERSONALITIES

Writers who publish under more than one name.

Most of the many writers who publish under more than one name are those producing genre fiction. They frequently adopt different names for different series of books, suggesting that their readers acquire their books for the subject matter rather than because they are a known and trusted author on any subject. For marketing purposes, prolific writers in various genres cannot always be seen to be 'churning out' too many books in a short time as this could devalue their work in the eyes of readers. But there are some notable examples among very well-known, literary-prize-winning authors. Sometimes, the disguise is very transparent – as with **Iain Banks** (mainstream fiction) and **Iain M. Banks** (science fiction). The acclaimed Irish writer, **John Banville**, takes on the name of **Benjamin Black** for his murder mysteries, while **Stephen King** has also written as **Richard Bachman** as his publisher felt that bringing out more than one book a year would devalue the brand. **Julian Barnes** is also the crime writer **Dan Kavanagh**, while Nobel laureate **Doris Lessing** used the name **Jane Somers** when she submitted *The Diary of a Good Neighbour* to a publisher – as a test of whether her work was being published because it was good, or whether it was simply because she was already famous. (It was actually published under the pseudonym.) **Cecil Day-Lewis** also wrote as **Nicholas Blake**, and **Gore Vidal** as **Edgar Box**. **J. K. Rowling** even changed sex to write as **Robert Galbraith**. And **Ruth Rendell** writes one kind of crime novel under her own name and another kind as **Barbara Vine**.

> **Talking Point**   Is there any point in writers adopting a different name for different genres when everyone knows who they are anyway?

SQUASHY BIG ARMCHAIR

Yes, that's the ideal armchair for reading in – large, deep, squashy, old, with a back high enough to rest your head against. If you're agile enough to literally 'curl up with a book', you'll want enough room to do so without getting cramp or pins and needles. The old-fashioned armchair with feather cushions beats anything chic or Scandinavian. And though sofas give you more room, they have one major drawback: others might sit on the sofa with you ... and they fidget.

STAFF RECOMMENDATIONS

Those little pieces of card, fixed to the shelves in bookshops, with nice hand-written recommendations from people who work there. It may be a cynical sales ploy, but it does at least throw a thread back to the time when nearly all booksellers were true enthusiasts and would actively promote to their customers books they themselves loved. Anyway, some of those who choose to work in bookshops, rather than sell designer goods at a higher salary, really do love books ... and are possibly even writing one themselves.

STREAM-OF-CONSCIOUSNESS

The term – first used by philosopher and psychologist William James (father of the famous novelist Henry James) – denotes the attempt to represent in writing the many thoughts, feelings, and fleeting perceptions that pass through a mind. Although closely related to **interior monologue**, it tends to be more diverse and appears to be less structured, recording every kind of thought, association and detail as it might occur.

The technique was pioneered by Dorothy Richardson (1873–1957) in her great, thirteen-volume *Pilgrimage* novel sequence (published 1915–1938), but it is a technique most famously associated with James Joyce's *Ulysses* (1922), with Virginia Woolf – especially *Mrs Dalloway* (1925) and *To the Lighthouse* (1927) – and with William Faulkner's *The Sound and the Fury* (1928).

T

Anthony Trollope – "Book love ... is your pass to the greatest, the purest, and the most perfect pleasure that God has prepared for his creatures."

TEN (FICTION) BOOKS TO READ BEFORE YOU DIE

If someone asked me, I would find it really, really hard. But if pushed, these would probably be my recommendations (in no order of priority). What would be yours?

1. *Don Quixote* by Miguel de Cervantes
2. *War and Peace* by Leo Tolstoy
3. *Anna Karenina* by Leo Tolstoy
4. *In Search of Lost Time* by Marcel Proust
5. *Mrs Dalloway* by Virginia Woolf
6. *Invisible Cities* by Italo Calvino
7. *The Portrait of a Lady* by Henry James
8. *Howards End* by E. M. Forster
9. *Middlemarch* by George Eliot
10. *Madame Bovary* by Gustave Flaubert

THIRD PERSON NARRATIVE

Stories told referring to the characters as 'she', 'he', or 'they'. The term derives from the traditional grammatical lay-out of verbs with 'I' as the first person singular, 'you' as the second person singular, 'he/she/it' as third person singular, 'we' as first person plural, 'you' as second person plural, and 'they' as third person plural. Third person narrative separates the voice of the narrator from the words and actions of the participants in the story and thus gives the illusion of some level of objectivity. It's a narrative mode more favoured in the past – think Jane Austen and George Eliot. (See also **Omniscient Narrator**.)

> **TALKING POINT** What are the advantages and/or disadvantages – for both reader and writer – of a story written in third person narrative?

TOTE BAGS

At one time it was only T-shirts: now it's just as likely to be linen tote bags – the way we declare to the world something about our identity, about how we want others to perceive us.

The confident book-lover will want to declare the tribe they belong to and send a message of recognition to other book-lovers. In a world where committed book-people are in the minority, it's like a secret handshake.

Bookshops have increasingly used the tote bag as a form of advertising, sometimes giving them away free – especially around Christmas when customers buy quite a lot of books at a time – sometimes selling them for a small amount, knowing that the true book-lover will want to declare their allegiance. Some shops are outlets for the Booksellers' Association tote bags that state in joyful orange letters, 'BOOKS ARE MY BAG'. Get one if you can. Don't be shy: flaunt it at every opportunity.

> **SUGGESTION** Use bookshop tote bags when you have to tackle the weekly shopping to remind yourself there is actually more to life than frozen peas, tea-bags and disinfectant.

TRANSLATION

… isn't merely a matter of knowing that the French say *la fenêtre* when we say 'window', et cetera. Translators have to be constantly alert to the cultural equivalents between languages, of subtle nuances of expression and reference that are the essence of literature. Give two translators the same even quite straightforward passage to translate and, chances are, they will come out differently. Here's the opening of the second volume of Marcel Proust's *In Search of Lost Time* (itself having an alternative translation as *Remembrance of Things Past*): first, as translated by C. K. Scott Moncrieff and Terence Kilmartin, revised by D. J. Enright (1992), then as translated by James Grieve (2002).

> My mother, when it was a question of our having M. de Norpois to dinner for the first time, having expressed her regret that Professor Cottard was away from home and that she herself had quite ceased to see anything of Swann …

> When it was first suggested we invite M. de Norpois to dinner, my mother commented that it was a pity Professor Cottard was absent from Paris and that she herself had quite lost touch with Swann …

Some of the greatest challenges for translators are colloquial expressions and 'expletives'. Some don't present too much of a problem: the French expression that translates literally as 'to sleep on both ears' can easily become 'to sleep like a log'. But we don't have the equivalent of the French expression 'to have Van Gogh's ear' – describing what your ear feels like after an over-long telephone conversation. And there's the problem of regional dialects: should a translator ignore the dialect and just translate it into standard English, or attempt an English equivalent and risk making the French speaker with a provincial accent sound as if they come from Cornwall or Liverpool ...

No wonder it takes years for translators to become experts at their job.

TRANSLATORS

Surely *the* most underappreciated workers in the literary world. Just imagine: without them we would never have made the acquaintance of Madame Bovary, Anna Karenina, or Don Quixote. We wouldn't all be able to read Dante's *Divine Comedy*, Dostoyevsky's *Crime and Punishment*, Tolstoy's *War and Peace*, the novels of Orhan Pamuk ... and thousands of other book in languages we can't speak. And the French, Germans and Russians wouldn't know the works of Shakespeare which, even in translation, they have long taken to their hearts.

It's rare to see the translator's name on the cover of a book: you will usually find it somewhere inside, but rarely given due prominence.

The skill, effort and dedication needed to turn a complex literary work into another language – usually for rather little payment – makes translators among the most generous, and selfless members of the publishing community. Praise them whenever you can.

TRAVEL WRITING

An increasingly popular genre with a long history, going back at least to the second century BCE with the *Description of Greece* by Pausanias, a traveller from Asia Minor who recorded his journeys in ten detailed volumes (some of the remains of what he described can still be seen today). Travel writing was also common in Mediaeval Arabic and Chinese literature. But the first important travel text in British literature was probably the *Voyages* of Hakluyt (1589). Another milestone was the publication, in 1784, of the diaries of Captain James Cook – an instant best-seller – though the slightly earlier *Journey to the Western Islands of Scotland* (1775) by Dr Johnson is better known today, along with the account of Johnson's friend and biographer, James Boswell, who published his *Journal of a Tour to the Hebrides* in 1786.

In the nineteenth century, the 'Grand Tour' produced many accounts of travels in Europe as young gentlemen completed their education by travelling. One lively variation on this is A. W. Kinglake's *Eothen* (1844), describing his travels in the Middle East as a young man, while Goethe's account of his *Italian Journey* (1816) is well worth seeking out – as are Dickens' *American Notes for General Circulation* (1842).

And here are some suggestions for books by outstanding recent travel writers:

Patrick Leigh Fermor (1915–2011): *A Time of Gifts* (1977).

Eric Newby (1919–2006): *A Short Walk in the Hindu Kush* (1958); *Round Ireland in Low Gear* (1987).

Jan Morris (b.1926): *Venice* (1960); *Trieste and the Meaning of Nowhere* (2001); *Europe – An Intimate Journey* (2006) – a wonderful collection of travel pieces.

Colin Thubron (b. 1939) *Among the Russians* (1983), *In Siberia* (1999); *Shadow of the Silk Road* (2006).

Bruce Chatwin (b.1940) *In Patagonia* (1977).

Paul Theroux (b.1941) *The Great Railway Bazaar* (1975); *Riding the Iron Rooster* (1988); *The Pillars of Hercules* (1995).

Bill Bryson (b.1951) *Neither Here Nor There: Travels in Europe* (1991); *Notes from a Small Island* (1995).

TYPO

Abbreviation for 'typographical error' – otherwise known as a misprint. Those irritating little mistakes in spelling or punctuation which shows the copy editor was momentarily distracted from checking the accuracy of the text. Some people get exceedingly irritated by these – and too many in one book can get tiresome and interrupt the flow of reading. But stop and think what a complex, detailed task it is to check every single word, every single full stop, comma, space, bracket etc etc. Please don't waste precious reading time by writing to inform the publisher that on page 276 (sixth line of third paragraph) 'them' should be 'then'. If *you* have realised it should be 'then', so will other readers. And can you honestly say you've never sent an email or written a letter with a small mistake in it? Did the sky fall on your head? Sense of proportion, please.

U

Miguel de Unanumo – "Art distils sensations and embodies them with enhanced meaning."

ULYSSES

Detractors like to call this masterpiece by James Joyce 'the greatest novel never read' – possibly because they can't be bothered to read it themselves. Those who have read it and love it know it's a very, very great novel – and I'm not talking about the size of it.

Purloining the title of Homer's great epic (Ulysses is the Roman version of the Greek Odysseus), Joyce seems both to suggest that the events of the day are a modern equivalent of the original 'Odyssey' and to make an ironic comparison between them. If you know your Homer, you will (possibly) spot the way various sections of Joyce's text echo incidents in the Ancient Greek story. But even if you don't, the pleasures to be got from the book are enormous.

The three principal characters are Ulysses/Odysseus (Leopold Bloom, son of Jewish emigrés), his wife Penelope (Molly Bloom) and his son Telemachus (Stephen Dedalus – a character first met as the protagonist in Joyce's *Portrait of the Artist as a Young*

Man – the metaphorical, rather than biological, son of Bloom whose actual son died in infancy).

Written between 1914 and 1921, it wasn't published in its entirety until 1922 when Sylvia Beach, the American who ran the original Shakespeare & Company bookshop in Paris, saw its significance as a great Modernist work and published it. Obscenity trials and bannings could not, however, keep a good book down for long.

If you don't feel up to reading it, there's a brilliant **audiobook** version recorded on the Naxos label, read by Jim Norton … with Marcia Riordan as Molly Bloom.

UNAUTHORISED BIOGRAPHY

Most reputable biographies have been given approval by the subject or the subject's estate, and they will generally co-operate with the biographer by providing access to useful materials such as letters, diaries, photographs, personal memories and introductions to other people who know/knew the subject.

An *unauthorised* biographer lacks this approval and co-operation. There are various possible reasons for the refusal to give approval, such as lack of confidence in the competence of the biographer, fear of revelations about – or interpretations of – incidents and relationships in the subject's life, or even an all-out disapproval of having any kind of biography written about them.

Although this is, in most ways, a disadvantage, the term 'unauthorised biography' has come to suggest, to some readers, the promise of the kind of juicy revelations that the subject or their family would rather remain unrevealed. Most serious readers will opt for authorised biographies – when available.

UNIVERSITY NOVEL, THE

Sometimes referred to as the 'Campus Novel', the University Novel became popular from the mid-twentieth century, the post-war expansion of higher education no doubt helping to provide a ready audience for stories of university life. Evelyn Waugh's *Brideshead Revisited* (1945) focuses mainly on students, whereas many famous later examples foreground the teaching staff. Satire is a frequent feature. Here are a few worth reading: *The Masters* (1951) by C. P. Snow; *Lucky Jim* (1954) by Kingsley Amis; *Pnin* (1957) by Vladimir Nabokov; *Porterhouse Blue* (1974) by Tom Sharpe; *Changing Places* (1975) and *Nice Work* (1988) by David Lodge; *The History Man* (1975) by Malcolm Bradbury; *Possession* (1990) by A. S. Byatt; *Disgrace* (1999) by J. M. Coetzee; *On Beauty* (2005) by Zadie Smith.

V

Voltaire – "You despise books, you whose lives are absorbed in the vanities of ambition, the pursuit of pleasure or indolence; but remember that all the known world, excepting only savage nations, is governed by books."

VALUE

It's very difficult to talk about 'value for money' with regard to books. Unlike painting, cheap reproductions are the same as the original. You don't need to be a millionaire to possess a great work of literature. *War and Peace* can be yours for the price of a cup of coffee – or for free if you're a library member.

VANDALISM

The most famous instance of book vandalism is that committed by playwright Joe Orton (1933–67) and his partner. They served six months in prison for altering images and blurbs on the covers of 72 library books and removing 1,653 plates from art books. Sticking the face of as monkey in the centre of a perfect English rose was one example of the vandalism they committed.

One might also regard books as having been vandalised when certain passages are removed on so-called moral grounds: in the past, many a school pupil has encountered major works of Greek and Roman literature in expurgated (or 'officially vandalised') versions.

The worst vandalism is, of course, to burn books (see **Book Burning**), but as Nobel laureate Joseph Brodsky pointed out, worse than burning books (or any other major or minor act of vandalism against them) is to leave them unread.

> **TALKING POINT** Does writing 'Very true' or 'Rubbish' in the margin of a book that doesn't actually belong to you constitute an act of vandalism?

VANITY PUBLISHING

At one time, if a would-be author was unable to secure a publisher for their work, they might resort to paying to have a book printed. They were 'vain' enough to believe it deserved publication – hence the term 'vanity publishing'. A number of companies cashed in on the vanity of these aspiring authors and provided a basic service but without the kind of promotion and publicity so essential for marketing the product. But it never had the kind of respectability conferred by 'proper' publishing.

But with the changes in the publishing industry (noted elsewhere in this book) and the difficulty of obtaining a worthwhile publishing contract, even writers previously with mainstream publishers are opting to finance publication themselves, especially as the internet and modern print technology make this relatively easy. 'Vanity publishing' has now largely been replaced by **self-publishing**.

VIRAGO

Founded in 1973, this ground-breaking publishing company was from the start dedicated to championing writing by women. In 1972, Rosie Boycott and Marsha Rowe had founded the feminist *Spare Rib* magazine, the launch of which was organised by the publicity company of Carmen Callil. It was Callil's idea to launch a publishing imprint, originally to be called 'Spare Rib Books'. In 1974, Boycott and Rowe left the team, to be replaced by Ursula Owen and Harriet Spicer. All have become legendary in the publishing world.

From the start, the books declared themselves to be part of the broader feminist project. In 1978, they launched the Virago Modern Classics series with Antonia White's *Frost in May*. Dedicated to the rediscovery of neglected women writers, they also published, in the same year, Vera Brittain's *Testament of Youth* which, as a result, became a television drama and subsequently a set text for school examinations. Since the early 80s, the company has passed into the hands of various big publishing groups but has managed to retain much of its original mission and continues to give us prize-winning and important books – both fiction and non-fiction – by women.

W

Jeanette Winterson – "Books work from the inside out. They are a private conversation happening somewhere in the soul."

WIGTOWN

Has, since 1998, been Scotland's 'national book town' (rather like Hay-on-Wye is for Wales). Home to more than twenty book-related businesses, offering over a quarter of a million books, old and new, it also hosts an excellent annual literature and arts festival for ten days each autumn. It offers nearly 200 events for adults and children, and has a very healthy festival 'fringe'.

WINDOW DISPLAYS

Those dominating displays of best-sellers and celebrity books in the windows of the big bookshops, they've been paid for by the publishers. Smaller publishers can't afford the fees and rely on the small, independent bookshops to display books they are truly enthusiastic about promoting.

WRITER

'The writer is someone who tears himself to pieces in order to liberate his neighbour.' Italo Calvino

WRITERS' BIRTHDAYS

Want the excuse for a party? Or just to raise a glass in homage to your favourite writers? Or to organise an event that highlights their work? (Or, if it's a writer you don't know, you could always use their birthday as a reason to find out about them.) Here are a few dates for your diary (and there's a much fuller list at the end of this book):

JANUARY Tolkien (3rd), Chekhov (17th), A. A. Milne (18th), Edgar Allan Poe (19th), Byron (22nd), Robert Burns and Virginia Woolf (25th), Lewis Carroll (27th).

FEBRUARY Muriel Spark (1st), James Joyce (2nd), Charles Dickens (7th), Jules Verne (8th), Boris Pasternak (10th), Georges Simenon (13th), Toni Morrison (18th), Carson McCullers (19th), Victor Hugo (26th), John Steinbeck (27th), Montaigne (28th).

MARCH Gabriel Garcia Marquez (6th), Tobias Smollett and John Updike (18th), Flannery O'Connor (25th), Maxim Gorky (28th), Gogol and John Fowles (31st).

APRIL Casanova, Hans Christian Andersen and Emile Zola (2nd), Wordsworth (7th), Samuel Beckett (13th), Henry James (15th), Charlotte Brontë (21st), Henry Fielding (22nd), Shakespeare and Vladimir Nabokov (23rd), Anthony Trollope (24th), Harper Lee (28th).

MAY   J. M. Barrie (9th), Daphne du Maurier (13th), Honoré de Balzac (20th), Sir Arthur Conan Doyle (22nd), Ian Fleming (28th).

JUNE   Thomas Hardy and the Marquis de Sade (2nd), Anne Frank (12th), Jean-Paul Sartre, Mary McCarthy and Françoise Sagan (21st), George Orwell (25th).

JULY   Franz Kafka and Tom Stoppard (3rd), Beatrix Potter (6th), Marcel Proust and Saul Bellow (10th), Wole Soyinka (13th), William Makepeace Thackeray and Yevgeny Yevtushenko (18th), Ernest Hemingway (21st), Aldous Huxley and Robert Graves (26th), Emily Brontë (30th).

AUGUST   James Baldwin (2nd), Percy Bysshe Shelley (4th), Alfred, Lord Tennyson (6th), John Galsworthy (14th), Sir Walter Scott (15th), Christopher Isherwood (26th), Mary Wollstonecraft (30th).

SEPTEMBER   Leo Tolstoy (9th), Agatha Christie (15th), H. G. Wells (21st), F. Scott Fitzgerald (24th), Elizabeth Gaskell (29th), Truman Capote (30th).

OCTOBER   Harold Pinter (10th), Katherine Mansfield (14th), Virgil (15th), Oscar Wilde (16th), Doris Lessing (22nd), Dylan Thomas (27th), John Keats (31st).

NOVEMBER   Fyodor Dostoyevsky (11th), Voltaire (21st), Louisa May Alcott (29th), Mark Twain (30th).

DECEMBER   Joseph Conrad (3rd), John Milton (9th), Gustave Flaubert (12th), Jane Austen (16th), Rudyard Kipling (30th).

WRITER'S BLOCK

A kind of creative constipation. Few known remedies. It's usually just a matter of time …

WRITERS' DIARIES

The diaries kept by writers often give a fascinating insight into the processes at work when they create their books, as well as into the circles in which they move – which are often very interesting in themselves. And because of the level of perceptiveness they bring to recording the world and events around them, their diaries can also be valuable to historians. Here are a few – by very contrasting writers (so there should be something for everyone) – that are well worth looking at.

The Journal of Beatrix Potter 1881–1897 – the diary she kept between the ages of fifteen and thirty, written in a code that was only cracked twenty years after her death.

Bernard Shaw: the Diaries 1885–1897 – not quite in code, but written in Pitman shorthand to maintain privacy.

A Writer's Diary 1877–1881 – by Fyodor Dostoyevsky is good if you're interested in Russian literature, or simply in history.

The Lewis Carroll Diaries – there are several volumes of these …

Journal – by Katherine Mansfield, has been called one of the classics of twentieth-century literature. Well worth reading for all sorts of reasons.

The Diaries of Franz Kafka – spanning 1910 to 1923. Not the jolliest of reads, but a valuable insight into the creator of some of the most original works of the twentieth century.

Chronicle of Youth – is Vera Brittain's diary of the Great War, covering 1913 to 1917.

A Writer's Diary – by Virginia Woolf. Extracts from the diaries she kept between 1918 and 1941, chosen by her husband, Leonard Woolf. A wonderful insight into both her life and her writing.

All My Road Before Me: The Diary of C. S. Lewis – kept between 1922 and 1927, covering his early years.

The Diary of Anaïs Nin – you may not want to tackle all seven volumes …

The Journals of Sylvia Plath 1950–1962 – good for getting behind all the mythology that has grown up around this writer since her suicide. A good antidote to those who emphasise the darker elements in her work. We meet the vibrant, life-affirming young woman.

The Orton Diaries – racy, honest and entertaining, they record the last eight months of playwright Joe Orton's life, before he was murdered by his long-term partner Kenneth Halliwell.

Untold Stories: The Alan Bennett Diaries – charming and entertaining … and a lot more besides.

WRITERS' GRAVES

Visiting writers' graves can be a form of **pilgrimage** – or just something to do, especially if you find yourself in Paris where there are three large cemeteries just stuffed with famous writers. In Britain, our writers tend to be more scattered across the country – apart from the very greatest who reside at **Poets' Corner** in Westminster Abbey – though in **Highgate Cemetery**, north London, you will find George Eliot,

Christina Rossetti, Karl Marx and Douglas Adams. On the cemetery island of **San Michele** in Venice, you'll find Ezra Pound and Joseph Brodsky. But here we go with those Parisian cities of the dead:

In **Père Lachaise** cemetery you'll find Apollinaire, Balzac, Beaumarchais, Alphonse Daudet, Colette, La Fontaine, Molière, Alfred de Musset, Gérard de Nerval, Georges Perec, Marcel Proust, Gertrude Stein and Alice B. Toklas, and Oscar Wilde. In **Montparnasse** cemetery are Charles Baudelaire, Eugene Ionesco, Jean-Paul Sartre and Simone de Beauvoir, Julio Cortázar, Susan Sontag, and Samuel Beckett. In the **Montmartre** cemetery are Alexandre Dumas *fils*, Théophile Gautier, Edmond and Jules de Goncourt, Claude Simon, Stendhal, and Alfred de Vigny.

WRITERS' LETTERS

Like writers' diaries, these can also provide an interesting insight into their lives and art. Writers as different as Virginia Woolf and Ernest Hemingway have had collections of their letters published. With 'great writers', it's sometimes hard to know how self-conscious their letter writing is: did they guess they might one day be collected and published? – and how might this have affected how they wrote and what they wrote about? (The same goes for their diaries, of course.)

X

Gao Xingjihan – "It's in literature that true
life can be found. It's under the mask of fiction
that you can tell the truth."

X

… is the kiss (literal or metaphorical) that a book-
lover bestows upon the giver of books or book tokens.

XENOPHILE

When it comes to reading, being a xenophile – a lover
of all things foreign – gives you access to wonderful
literature from the whole world, not just our little
island. And it's thanks to **translators** that we can
share so many pleasures.

The vast wealth of European literature is the newly
converted xenophile's first port of call, but further
pleasures await beyond the European borders – with
the rich literature of Turkey, for example. The current
success of Nobel laureate Orhan Pamuk grows out of a
long tradition of Turkish literature, which is blooming
even more prolifically in the twenty-first century.

Translations from Arabic are gradually becoming
more available, while authors from India, Japan and

China are also benefitting from our growing global consciousness – and contributing to it.

Two of the joys of reading literature from other cultures are the experience of what is different from our own lives and, even more importantly perhaps, the discovery of our commonality. Literature really can play a part in breaking down barriers between nations and dissolving prejudices born of ignorance. Readers, lead the way!

XMAS

The perfect excuse to give and receive books. The publishing industry relies on this festival of generosity to support its existence, a large percentage of its annual trade 'happening' at this season. (Keep it up!)

Y

Yevgeny Yevtushenko – "A poet's autobiography is his poetry. Anything else is just a footnote."

YOU

… dear Reader.

YOUNG ADULT

Young Adult – or YA – is a recognised library and publishing category that indicates books written specifically for adolescents and young adults – though many are, apparently, bought by readers over 18, too. Not surprisingly, most YA novels feature protagonists within the same age group as the target readers and concern issues and situations of particular relevance to that time of life. Such novels started to come particularly to the fore in the 1960s and 1970s (perhaps in response to more child-centred education), S. E. Hinton's *The Outsiders* (1967) being the first outstanding example.

YA fiction can be an important staging post between childhood reading and tackling fully adult books, which are often too demanding in style, complexity and subject matter for young people – particularly those who lack confidence in reading. But they also provide a useful forum for young people to explore issues of particular relevance to their lives and the difficulties they may encounter – as well as promoting the experience of reading itself as a valuable and useful activity, which it is hoped they will take forward into adult life.

Z

Carlos Ruiz Zafón – "The Cemetery of Forgotten Books is like the greatest, most fantastic library you could ever imagine. It's a labyrinth of books with tunnels, bridges, arches, secret sections ..."

ZERO-RATED

This is a VAT (Value Added Tax) term indicating that a product is not liable for that tax. Zero-rated products currently include books. From time to time, governments have proposed changing this situation. Hopefully, they will continue to fear the power of writers to get their own back through the printed word if such a proposal were to be implemented. It is up to all book-lovers to resist such a move, on behalf of civilisation.

Zzzzzzzzzzz

So, you've fallen asleep over your book again. Never mind. It's a lovely way to end the day!

WRITERS' BIRTHDAYS

In case you want to raise a glass to one of your favourites …

January

1	E. M. Forster	22	Lord Byron
3	J. R. R. Tolkien		Auguste Strindberg
6	E. L. Doctorow	23	Derek Walcott
7	Gerald Durrell		Edith Wharton
8	Wilkie Collins	25	Robert Burns
9	Simone de Beauvoir		Somerset Maugham
12	Jack London		Virginia Woolf
14	John Dos Passos	27	Lewis Carroll
17	Anton Chekhov	28	Colette
18	A. A. Milne	31	Norman Mailer
19	Julian Barnes		
	Edgar Allan Poe		

February

1	Muriel Spark	18	Toni Morrison
2	James Joyce		Nikos Kazantzakis
3	Gertrude Stein	19	Carson McCullers
6	Christopher Marlowe	21	W. H. Auden
7	Charles Dickens	23	Samuel Pepys
	Sinclair Lewis	25	Anthony Burgess
	Laura Ingalls Wilder	26	Victor Hugo
8	Jules Verne	27	Lawrence Durrell
10	Boris Pasternak		John Steinbeck
13	Georges Simenon		Longfellow
16	Angela Carter	28	Michel de Montaigne

March

4	Alan Sillitoe	20	Heinrik Ibsen
6	Elizabeth Barrett-Browning	24	William Morris
	Gabriel Garcia Marquez	25	Flannery O'Connor
		26	Robert Frost
10	James Herriot		A. E. Housman
12	Edward Albee		Tennessee Williams
18	Tobias Smollett	28	Maxim Gorky
	Stéphane Mallarmé	30	Paul Verlaine
	John Updike	31	John Fowles
19	Philip Roth		Nikolai Gogol
			Sean O'Casey

April

2	Hans Christian Andersen	16	Kingsley Amis
	Casanova		Anatole France
	Emile Zola		J. M. Synge
4	Maya Angelou	17	Isak Dinesen (Karen Blixen)
	Marguerite Duras		Thornton Wilder
5	Algernon Swinburne	21	Charlotte Brontë
7	William Wordsworth	22	Henry Fielding
9	Charles Baudelaire	23	Vladimir Nabokov
10	Paul Theroux		William Shakespeare
12	Johanna Spyri	24	Anthony Trollope
13	Samuel Beckett	25	Walter De La Mare
15	Eva Figes	26	Mary Wollstonecraft
	Henry James	28	Harper Lee
		30	Alice B. Toklas

May

1	Joseph Heller	25	Edward Bulwer-Lytton
5	Karl Marx		Theodore Roethke
6	Sigmund Freud	27	John Barth
7	Robert Browning		John Cheever
8	Thomas Pynchon		Dashiell Hammett
9	J. M. Barrie	28	Ian Fleming
12	Edward Lear		Walker Percy
13	Bruce Chatwin		Patrick White
	Alphonse Daudet	29	G. K. Chesterton
	Daphne du Maurier		T. H. White
17	Dorothy Richardson	31	Walt Whitman
20	Honoré de Balzac		
21	Alexander Pope		
22	Sir Arthur Conan Doyle		
24	Joseph Brodsky		
	Mikhail Sholokov		

June

1	John Masefield	20	Lillian Hellman
2	Thomas Hardy	21	Mary McCarthy
	Marquis de Sade		Françoise Sagan
10	Maurice Sendak		Jean-Paul Sartre
11	Ben Johnson	22	Erich Maria Remarque
	William Styron	23	Jean Anouilh
12	Djuna Barnes	25	George Orwell
	Anne Frank	26	Pearl S. Buck
13	Dorothy L. Sayers	28	Luigi Pirandello
	W. B. Yeats		Jean-Jacques Rousseau
14	Harriet Beecher Stowe	29	Antoine de
16	Joyce Carol Oates		Saint-Exupéry
19	Salman Rushdie	30	Czeslaw Milosz

July

1	George Sand	18	William Makepeace
2	Hermann Hesse		Thackeray
3	Franz Kafka		Yevgeny Yevtushenko
	Tom Stoppard	19	A. J. Cronin
4	Nathaniel Hawthorne	20	Petrarch
5	Jean Cocteau	21	Ernest Hemingway
6	Beatrix Potter	23	Raymond Chandler
8	La Fontaine	24	Alexandre Dumas *père*
10	Saul Bellow	25	Elias Canetti
	Marcel Proust	26	Robert Graves
12	Pablo Neruda		Aldous Huxley
13	Wole Soyinka	27	Alexandre Dumas *fils*
14	Isaac Bashevis Singer	28	Gerard Manley Hopkins
17	Christina Stead	30	Emily Brontë

August

1	Herman Melville	18	Alain Robbe-Grillet
2	James Baldwin	19	Ogden Nash
3	P. D. James	22	Dorothy Parker
4	Knut Hamsun	24	Jorge Luis Borges
	Percy Bysshe Shelley	25	Martin Amis
5	Guy de Maupassant		V. S. Naipaul
6	Alfred, Lord Tennyson	26	John Buchan
9	John Dryden		Christopher Isherwood
11	Alex Haley	27	Theodore Dreiser
	Charlotte M. Yonge		C. S. Forester
14	John Galsworthy	28	Johann Wolfgang von
15	T. E. Lawrence		Goethe
	Sir Walter Scott	29	Oliver Wendell Holmes
16	Georgette Heyer	30	Mary Wollstonecraft
17	Ted Hughes	31	William Saroyan

September

3	Alison Lurie	18	Dr. Samuel Johnson
4	Chateaubriand	20	Upton Sinclair
	Mary Renault	21	H. G. Wells
5	Arthur Koestler	24	F. Scott Fitzgerald
7	Malcolm Bradbury		Horace Walpole
	Edith Sitwell	25	William Faulkner
8	Alfred Jarry	26	T. S. Eliot
	Siegfried Sassoon	28	Prosper Merimée
9	Leo Tolstoy		Stephen Spender
10	Hilda Doolittle	29	Elizabeth Gaskell
13	Sherwood Anderson	30	Truman Capote
	J. B. Priestley		
15	Agatha Christie		
17	Mary Stewart		
	William Carlos Williams		

October

2	Wallace Stevens	18	Thomas Love Peacock
	Jan Morris	19	John le Carré
3	Thomas Wolfe	20	Arthur Rimbaud
	Gore Vidal	21	Samuel Taylor Coleridge
5	Denis Diderot		
10	Harold Pinter	22	Doris Lessing
14	Katherine Mansfield	25	Zadie Smith
	e.e. cummings	27	Dylan Thomas
15	Virgil	28	Evelyn Waugh
	C. P. Snow	29	James Boswell
16	Oscar Wilde	30	Richard Brinsley Sheridan
	Eugene O'Neill		
	Günther Grass	31	John Evelyn
17	Arthur Miller		John Keats

November

3	André Malraux	21	Beryl Bainbridge
6	Thomas Kyd		Voltaire
	Robert Musil	22	André Gide
7	Albert Camus	24	Laurence Sterne
8	Kazuo Ishiguro	25	Leonard Woolf
9	Ivan Turgenev	28	John Bunyan
10	Friedrich von Schiller		William Blake
11	Fyodor Dostoyevsky	29	Louisa May Alcott
	Kurt Vonnegut		C. S. Lewis
13	Robert Louis Stevenson	30	Jonathan Swift
18	Margaret Atwood		Mark Twain
	Wyndham Lewis		
20	Thomas Chatterton		
	Nadine Gordimer		

December

3	Joseph Conrad	16	Jane Austen
4	Rainer Maria Rilke		Noël Coward
5	Christina Rossetti	17	Ford Madox Ford
	Joan Didion		Erskine Caldwell
6	Kalil Gibran	18	Saki (H.H.Munro)
7	Willa Cather	19	Jean Genet
8	Horace	21	Heinrich Böll
9	John Milton	22	Jean-Baptiste Racine
10	Emily Dickinson	24	Matthew Arnold
	Rumer Godden	25	Rebecca West
11	Alfred de Musset	26	Thomas Gray
	Alexander Solzhenitsyn		Henry Miller
12	Gustave Flaubert	30	Rudyard Kipling
13	Heinrich Heine		

Heather Reyes

AN EVERYWHERE

a little book about reading

During several months of treatment for a serious illness, the writer decides to turn a necessary evil into an opportunity: the luxury of reading whatever takes her fancy.

An Everywhere: a little book about reading is a quietly passionate and witty defence of the joys and consolations of reading in both the difficult and day-to-day aspects of our lives.

'A brilliant travel guide to the city of book: the city we hold within us, and the one we share with all its other citizens. I love ... the blend of erudition and intimacy she brings to the discussion of what reading is and what books can do within a life. It is such a truthful book, honest about panic and anguish, and fascinating about what happens when the panic ebbs and the reader continues.'   Helen Dunmore

'*An Everywhere* is an extended love letter to the joys of reading and a celebration of the book as a physical object. An illuminating and often moving guide to an individual's relationship with the written word.'
W B Gooderham, *The Guardian*

Available in ebook/print book   £8.99   978 099263640 1
Available from all good bookshops

Oxygen Books

www.oxygenbooks.co.uk

'Hugely readable and quietly profound ... lyrical and deeply moving.'   Beatrice Colin

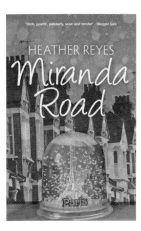

Miranda Road
Heather Reyes

Once she dreamt of literary fame, now Georgina Hardiman just tries to bring up her young daughter Eloisa intelligently – and to stay sane in Thatcher's Britain.

But Eloisa has her own ideas about what she wants from life ... starting with a father.

A visit to Paris brings mother and daughter up against secrets of the past – and starts them both on a journey towards different kinds of happiness.

Miranda Road is a bitter-sweet and wonderfully witty meditation on love, on being a mother and a daughter, and on the difficulties of freeing ourselves from the past.

'Rich, poetic, painterly, wise and tender – Heather Reyes portrays the last half-century of a changing Europe but also fictionalises the life of a mother and writer who loves her daughter and loves words, and manages to send both into the future'   Maggie Gee

Available in ebook/print book   £8.99   978 099263641 8
Available from all good bookshops

Oxygen Books
www.oxygenbooks.co.uk